Dreamweaver CS6 Mobile and Web Development with HTML5, CSS3, and jQuery Mobile

Harness the cutting-edge features of Dreamweaver for mobile and web development

David Karlins

PUBLISHING

BIRMINGHAM - MUMBAI

Dreamweaver CS6 Mobile and Web Development with HTML5, CSS3, and jQuery Mobile

First published: May 2013

Production Reference: 1150513

Published by Packt Publishing Ltd.
Livery Place
35 Livery Street
Birmingham B3 2PB, UK.

ISBN 978-1-84969-474-2

www.packtpub.com

Cover Image by Suresh Mogre (suresh.mogre.99@gmail.com)

Credits

Author
David Karlins

Reviewers
Nelson Therrien

Chris Valleskey

Acquisition Editors
Wilson D'Souza

Rukhsana Khambatta

Lead Technical Editor
Mayur Hule

Technical Editors
Dominic Pereira

Dennis John

Copy Editors
Alfida Paiva

Insiya Morbiwala

Laxmi Subramanian

Sajeev Raghavan

Aditya Nair

Project Coordinator
Abhishek Kori

Proofreader
Mario Cecere

Indexer
Rekha Nair

Production Coordinator
Nilesh R. Mohite

Cover Work
Nilesh R. Mohite

About the Author

David Karlins is a web design consultant, teacher, and author of dozens of books on web design, including *Building Websites All-in-One For Dummies, John Wiley & Sons Inc.* (co-author with Doug Sahlin), *Adobe Creative Suite 5 Web Premium How-Tos: 100 Essential Techniques, Peachpit,* and *Dreamweaver CS5.5 Mobile and Web Development with HTML5, CSS3, and jQuery, Packt Publishing.*

Thanks to my agent Margot Hutchinson and everyone at Packt Publishing for their role in bringing this book to life. And I want to express special appreciation to Richard Jørgensen who provided expert input and review for this book.

About the Reviewers

Nelson Therrien has computer degrees in both multimedia and programming. He is an Adobe Certified Expert (ACE) with Dreamweaver and has many Brainbench certifications (HTML, XHTML, Dreamweaver, Flash, Web design, Photoshop).

Most of his time is spent teaching and developing web applications and dynamic forms. He is teaching at Eliquo, Canada's biggest Apple- and Adobe-authorized training center. He's responsible for everything that revolves around the Web at the Montreal office.

You would see his reference if you were to take a course on Dreamweaver, Flash, ActionScript, Flex, ColdFusion, HTML5, CSS3, XML, JavaScript, jQuery, PHP, LiveCycle Designer, or accessibility and standards on the Web. He has also touched on ASP, .NET, Java, SQL, Photoshop, Fireworks, and Illustrator.

He spoke at the launch of Adobe CS5 and CS5.5 in Canada as an Eliquo representative.

He is also the father of three young children aged between three and six.

As a way to relax, he's constantly reading and searching to improve his skills and knowledge, and he does find some time to play Canada's national game: hockey! He's a goaltender and coaches his two sons.

I'd like to thank Craig Boassaly, Eliquo's president, and the team at Eliquo for making my teaching job so much fun.

I'd also like to thank my wife who takes care of our three angels when I'm too busy to help her. And I'd like to thank my three kids Josué, Isaac, and Kaïla for bringing so much sunshine into my life. Lastly, I'd like to thank God: nothing that I have in this world or that I'll have in the next would be without Him.

Chris Valleskey is a young and creative thinker who currently lives in Chicago, IL. He started freelancing at the age of 17 and continued this role throughout college until graduating in 2011 with a Bachelor of Arts in Graphic Design and Philosophy. Although he now holds a normal job in the city, he also enjoys spending time with his close friends as a part owner in their own company. In his free time, he enjoys playing Halo, drinking Mountain Dew, and hanging out with his awesome wife.

I would like to especially thank my wife Krista for putting up with me, and for my friends and family for supporting and encouraging me in everything I do.

www.PacktPub.com

Support files, eBooks, discount offers and more

You might want to visit www.PacktPub.com for support files and downloads related to your book.

Did you know that Packt offers eBook versions of every book published, with PDF and ePub files available? You can upgrade to the eBook version at www.PacktPub.com and as a print book customer, you are entitled to a discount on the eBook copy. Get in touch with us at service@packtpub.com for more details.

At www.PacktPub.com, you can also read a collection of free technical articles, sign up for a range of free newsletters and receive exclusive discounts and offers on Packt books and eBooks.

http://PacktLib.PacktPub.com

Do you need instant solutions to your IT questions? PacktLib is Packt's online digital book library. Here, you can access, read and search across Packt's entire library of books.

Why Subscribe?

- Fully searchable across every book published by Packt
- Copy and paste, print and bookmark content
- On demand and accessible via web browser

Free Access for Packt account holders

If you have an account with Packt at www.PacktPub.com, you can use this to access PacktLib today and view nine entirely free books. Simply use your login credentials for immediate access.

Table of Contents

Preface

This book goes to press at a time of radical developments in the evolution of web design. Mobile design is no longer an afterthought but integral to the process of building websites from conception to completion. New features in HTML5, CSS3, and JavaScript have eclipsed older technologies for animation and interactivity. Native video has supplanted plugin-based media. Moreover, new HTML5 and CSS3 tools have brought about a sea of change in everything from form design to graphical styling.

Dreamweaver CS6 addresses these new demands, and this book shows you how to take maximum advantage of new features and how to repurpose established Dreamweaver features to solve new design challenges.

For readers new to Dreamweaver, this book provides a solid, compressed introduction to the essential building blocks for creating cutting-edge and stable sites. For experienced Dreamweaver designers, this book explains how to take advantage of the new features available in CS6 in detail, with particular focus on new features for designing mobile sites in jQuery Mobile and for generating apps.

This book starts off by teaching you how to create web pages in Dreamweaver using the latest technology and approaches—HTML5, CSS3, and JavaScript. It demonstrates how to create or customize pages with HTML5 layouts and add HMTL5 native audio and video to these pages. Then you will learn to add CSS3 effects to web pages using Dreamweaver, and sometimes push beyond the features available in Dreamweaver.

The later chapters of the book focus on mobile design. The book covers Dreamweaver CS6's tools for responsive design, to adjust the display to match a user's device, to learn how to build jQuery-based web apps, and to learn how to convert those web apps to free-standing apps that run without a browser. By the time you're finished, you'll have learned several techniques to use the latest features of Dreamweaver for web and mobile development.

What this book covers

Chapter 1, Creating Sites and Pages with Dreamweaver CS6, provides a compressed overview and introduction to Dreamweaver CS6, including defining a site, creating HTML5 pages, applying tags with the Properties inspector, defining links, inserting images, linking to external stylesheets, and designing pages with ID and class div tags.

Chapter 2, Using HTML5 for Page Structure, explores how to build web pages by relying on new, standardized semantic page structuring elements in HTML5, including `<header>`, `<nav>`, `<article>`, `<section>`, `<aside>`, and `<footer>`.

Chapter 3, Collecting Data with Forms, covers generating client-side (JavaScript) forms for navigation, defining forms with Spry validation fields, applying HTML5 parameters to form fields, styling forms, and connecting forms with real-world server applications.

Chapter 4, Applying CSS3 Effects and Transforms, covers shadows, border radius, and opacity; designing with CSS3 transform; and creating animation with CSS3 and Dreamweaver animation tools.

Chapter 5, Embedding HTML5 Native Audio and Video, is about preparing, embedding, and testing native audio and video.

Chapter 6, Responsive Design with Media Queries, discusses defining stylesheets to customize the display in laptops, tablets, and smartphones.

Chapter 7, Creating Mobile Pages with jQuery Mobile, is about creating pages based on jQuery Mobile—accessible, inviting, and animated pages that work particularly well in mobile devices.

Chapter 8, Enhancing Mobile Sites, discusses adding layout grids, collapsible blocks, and mobile-friendly forms.

Chapter 9, Customizing Themes with ThemeRoller, covers applying jQuery Mobile themes with Dreamweaver CS6 swatches, customizing themes with ThemeRoller, and applying custom themes.

Chapter 10, Building Apps with PhoneGap, delves into publishing mobile apps for iOS (iPhone, iPod Touch, and iPad) and Android devices using new tools in Dreamweaver 6.

What you need for this book

To work through this book most effectively, you need access to Dreamweaver CS6 or higher. However, the book includes tips and notes to enable designers using earlier versions of Dreamweaver, right back till Version 3, to take advantage of Adobe-provided tools for creating HTML5-based and CSS3-based websites.

Who this book is for

This book is apt for experienced Dreamweaver web designers looking to migrate to HTML5 and jQuery. It also targets web designers new to Dreamweaver who want to jump with two feet into the most current web design tools and features. While focusing primarily on Dreamweaver CS6, this book includes content of value to readers using older versions of Dreamweaver, with directions on installing a version of Adobe's HTML5 Pack that updates those packages.

Conventions

In this book, you will find a number of styles of text that distinguish between different kinds of information. Here are some examples of these styles, and an explanation of their meaning.

Code words in text, database table names, folder names, filenames, file extensions, pathnames, dummy URLs, user input, and Twitter handles are shown as follows: "As this is going to be a one-page site, the `index.html` filename will open the page when the site's URL is addressed in a browser."

A block of code is set as follows:

```
<div data-role="collapsible" data-collapsed="true">

    <h3>Header</h3>
  <p>Content</p>
</div>
```

New terms and **important words** are shown in bold. Words that you see on the screen, in menus or dialog boxes for example, appear in the text like this: "Doing this opens the **Select Image Source** dialog."

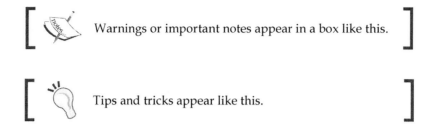

Warnings or important notes appear in a box like this.

Tips and tricks appear like this.

Reader feedback

Feedback from our readers is always welcome. Let us know what you think about this book—what you liked or may have disliked. Reader feedback is important for us to develop titles that you really get the most out of.

To send us general feedback, simply send an e-mail to feedback@packtpub.com, and mention the book title via the subject of your message.

If there is a topic that you have expertise in and you are interested in either writing or contributing to a book, see our author guide on www.packtpub.com/authors.

Customer support

Now that you are the proud owner of a Packt book, we have a number of things to help you to get the most from your purchase.

Errata

Although we have taken every care to ensure the accuracy of our content, mistakes do happen. If you find a mistake in one of our books—maybe a mistake in the text or the code—we would be grateful if you would report this to us. By doing so, you can save other readers from frustration and help us improve subsequent versions of this book. If you find any errata, please report them by visiting http://www.packtpub.com/submit-errata, selecting your book, clicking on the **errata submission form** link, and entering the details of your errata. Once your errata are verified, your submission will be accepted and the errata will be uploaded on our website, or added to any list of existing errata, under the Errata section of that title. Any existing errata can be viewed by selecting your title from http://www.packtpub.com/support.

Piracy

Piracy of copyright material on the Internet is an ongoing problem across all media. At Packt, we take the protection of our copyright and licenses very seriously. If you come across any illegal copies of our works, in any form, on the Internet, please provide us with the location address or website name immediately so that we can pursue a remedy.

Please contact us at `copyright@packtpub.com` with a link to the suspected pirated material.

We appreciate your help in protecting our authors, and our ability to bring you valuable content.

Questions

You can contact us at `questions@packtpub.com` if you are having a problem with any aspect of the book, and we will do our best to address it.

1

Creating Sites and Pages with Dreamweaver CS6

This book covers, in a compressed way, the whole range of cutting edge and advanced features available in Dreamweaver CS6. Our emphasis is on the new features in HTML5 that structure content and make it more accessible, on CSS3 styles that add transformations (such as rotations) and effects (such as rounded corners) to elements, and on mobile design with HTML5 Media Queries and jQuery Mobile. Dreamweaver CS6 provides all the important tools for implementing all these features.

We'll get to that very shortly. But first, in this chapter, it will be important to review (and for those of you new to Dreamweaver, understand) some fundamental tools for maximizing productivity in Dreamweaver. Doing this serves two purposes: it provides a fast-and-furious overview of the basics of Dreamweaver CS6, and probably more importantly, it grounds us all in the protocols that protect the integrity of everything else that we are going to cover in this book.

In this chapter, we will:

- Define a Dreamweaver site
- Create HTML5 pages
- Apply elements to text
- Define links
- Insert images
- Create CSS files and link HTML pages to those stylesheets
- Define and apply ID and class Div styles for page design

Defining a Dreamweaver site

Everything you do in Dreamweaver requires that you first create a Dreamweaver site. Without that Dreamweaver site, nothing really works in Dreamweaver.

Why is that? Basically, this is because the web pages you learn to build in the course of this book involve dozens of files. Dozens? Really? Well, count them: a few JavaScript files, links to internal and external pages, embedded audios, videos, and images, links to CSS files, and embedded content from other pages using the iFrame technique. We're up to dozens already!

If any of the relationships or links between these files gets corrupted — through a file being moved, renamed, or deleted — our page collapses. But if we are working within (and following the rules for working in) a Dreamweaver site, Dreamweaver keeps track of all the files in all your web pages — for example, embedded image files and video clips and links to other web pages — and makes sure all those files work together.

A Dreamweaver site also provides tools to manage file transfers between our local (preview) site and the online remote version of the site.

Defining a local site

All this starts with defining a separate (and just one) Dreamweaver *Site* for every website you manage with Dreamweaver. We have "*Site*" in italics and capitalized here to emphasize that we are not talking about organizing files in a "website", but defining a very specific Dreamweaver thing — a Site.

The easiest way to do that from any interface in Dreamweaver is through the **Site** menu. And the first (and only essential) part of defining a site is to create a local version on your own computer; linkage to a remote (online) server can come later.

Before defining a Dreamweaver site, create a folder on your computer (your desktop is a convenient place) that will serve as the root folder for your site. Avoid spaces or special characters while naming that folder (that is, `daves-website` not `Dave's Website!`).

To define a local site, follow these steps:

1. With Dreamweaver CS6 launched, choose **Site | New Site**. The **Site Setup** dialog opens.

2. In the **Site Name** field, enter any content that helps you distinguish this site from other sites. There are no constraints on using spaces or special characters.

3. In the **Local Site Folder** field, use the **Browse for Folder** icon to locate the folder you created to serve as your site's root folder.

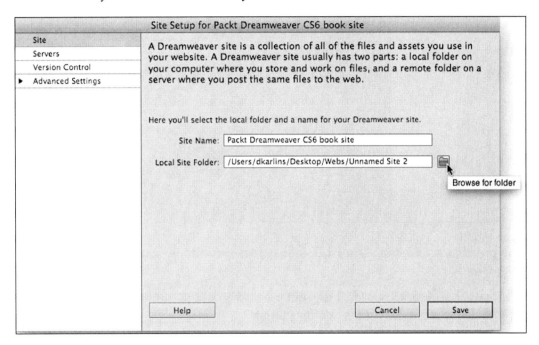

The preceding screenshot shows how to create a root folder for a Dreamweaver site.

4. After you click on the **Browse for Folder** icon, the **Choose Root Folder** dialog opens. Navigate to your root folder and click on **Choose**. This returns you to the **Site Setup** dialog.

5. Click on **Save** to complete the local site's definition:

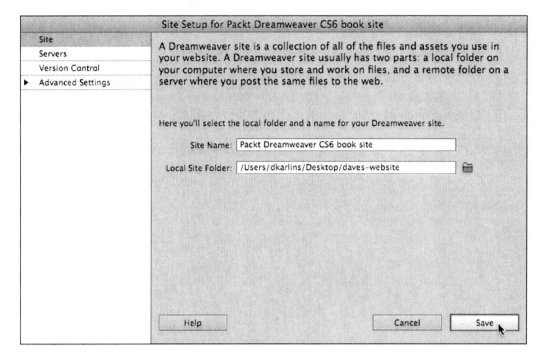

The previous screenshot shows a Dreamweaver site with the **Local Site Folder** file defined.

We'll return shortly to our local site and see how to use it, but first let's walk through how to define a remote connection for our site.

Defining a remote site

Most websites are intended for public distribution on the Internet. They are hosted on servers that enable this; these server hosts are easy to find (one reliable list of pricing and features is at `http://reviews.cnet.com/web-hosting-plans/`).

You need to have contracted for remote hosting before you can define a Dreamweaver CS6 link to a remote server. This hosting service will provide you with three essential pieces of information—an FTP address, a username, and a password. Some hosting setups include a defined root directory as well. Record that information when you contract for hosting, or look up the login info for your current hosting service if you are incorporating that server into a Dreamweaver site only now.

With your FTP address, username, and password taken care of, the following steps walk through what is required to define a remote connection for your Dreamweaver site. Or don't. Remember, a remote site is not necessary to build a site on your own computer, and you'll be able to work through almost everything in this book without a remote connection.

To define a remote connection for a Dreamweaver site, follow these steps:

1. With Dreamweaver CS6 launched, choose **Site | Manage Sites**. This opens the **Manage Sites** dialog, and by the way, you use this technique (managing a site) to edit anything in your Dreamweaver site definition, not just the remote connection.

2. In the **Manage Sites** dialog, double-click on your site from the **Your Sites** list to open the **Site Setup** dialog again.

3. In the list of categories on the left-hand side of the **Site Setup** dialog, select **Servers**.

4. Click on the **Add New Server (+)** button. Another dialog named **Site Setup...** opens.

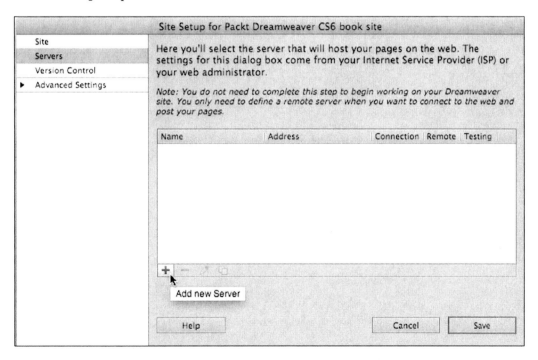

The previous screenshot shows a new server connection being added to a site definition.

5. In the **Server Name** field, enter any text that helps you remember what server you are connecting to.

6. In the **FTP Address** field, enter the FTP address provided by your hosting administrator, in the **Username** field enter the provided username, and in the **Password** field enter your password. Most sites use **Port 21**, so don't change the default value in the **Port** field unless instructed by your site administrator.

7. Selecting the **Use Passive FTP** and **Use FTP Performance Optimization** checkboxes can be advantageous in avoiding connection glitches. To see these options, expand the **More Options** section of the **Site Setup...** dialog. By default, these checkboxes are selected in Dreamweaver CS6.

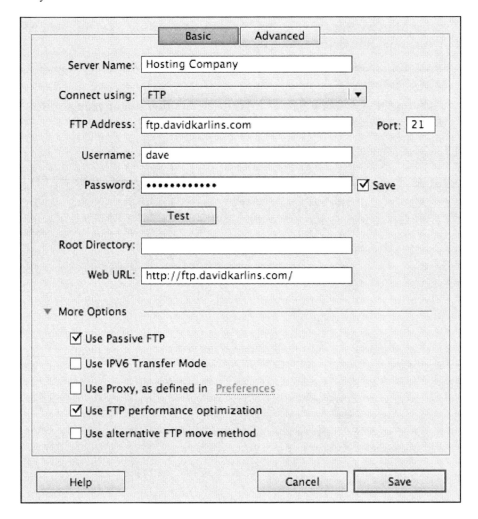

The preceding screenshot illustrates a defined remote connection.

8. The **Web URL** field is filled in automatically by Dreamweaver based on what you enter in the **FTP Address** field. This information is used by Dreamweaver for tools such as its built-in, link-checking features, but it is not relevant to, and serves more as a distraction from the process of defining a site. If you wish, you can replace the generated URL with the actual URL for your website.

9. Don't click on **Save** yet. First, click on the **Test** button. If you get an error message, check your FTP address, login credentials, and password with your site-hosting company (and be sure you are connected to the Internet). When the **Test** button produces a message saying that you have connected to your web server successfully, click on **Save**.

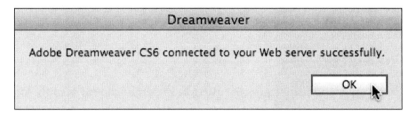

The preceding screenshot illustrates a successfully tested remote connection.

10. After you save the remote connection, the **Site Setup ...** dialog reappears. Click on **Save** again. Then, click on the **Done** button in the **Manage Sites** dialog. Your site is now defined!

Transferring files between a local and remote site

After you define a Dreamweaver site, you can view files in either the local or remote version of the site in the **Files** panel. Like any other panel in Dreamweaver, you can view or hide the **Files** panel through the **Window** menu.

There are two drop-down menus in the toolbar at the top of the **Files** panel. Use the first one to select a Dreamweaver site. If you have only one site, that site will be selected by default.

The second drop-down menu in the **Files** toolbar toggles between four views, two of which are relevant and two of which are esoteric for most designers. The first two options toggle between viewing files on the local or remote versions of the site. The **Testing server** option is for backend programming scripts, which manage data, and the **Repository view** option is for stored code snippets.

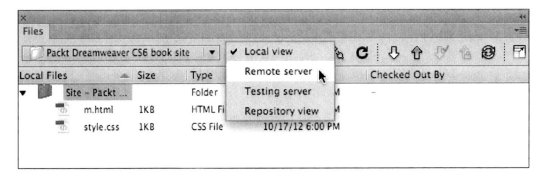

The preceding screenshot illustrates toggling between local and remote views.

When you click on the **Connect to Remote Server** button, you can use the **Files** panel to view files in your remote site. You can split the **Files** panel by clicking on the **Expand/Collapse** icon at the far right of the **Files** panel toolbar:

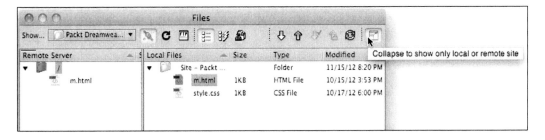

In the preceding screenshot, the **Connect to Remote Server** button is pressed, and the **Collapse/Expand** button is hovered over; this allows us to toggle between viewing both local and remote views together, (when expanded) or only the local or remote view (when collapsed).

You can drag files from the local to remote sides of the **Files** panel, or use the **Get Files** (down arrow) or **Put Files** (up arrow) notation to download or upload your files respectively.

Creating an HTML5 page

With a site defined, you are ready to create HTML5 pages in Dreamweaver. HTML5 is the current standard for HTML, and is also the most widely supported version of HTML, including the older browsers. There are some new features in HTML5 that are not supported by older browsers, but HTML5 documents produce per-se the fewest error messages for visitors using older browsers to view modern websites. For these reasons, HTML5 is the default document type for web pages in Dreamweaver CS6.

Dreamweaver CS6 comes with predesigned HTML5 page layouts, one for two-column pages, and one for three-column pages. These are useful and well documented, but we'll have to rush past them in this compressed introduction to Dreamweaver CS6 to get right to building HTML5 pages from scratch.

Follow these steps to create a new HTML5 page in Dreamweaver CS6:

1. Choose **File | New** from Dreamweaver's main menu. The **New Document** dialog appears.

2. From the left-hand side column, choose **Blank Page**. In the **Page Type** column, choose **HTML**. In the **Layout** column, choose **<none>**. And leave **HTML 5** as the setting in the **DocType** drop-down menu. Click on the **Create** button to generate a new page.

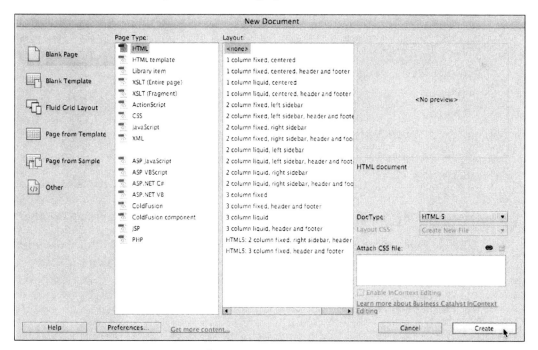

Creating a new HTML5 page

3. The new page opens in Dreamweaver's **Design** window. We won't explore every option in the **Design** window, but will identify key ones:

    ◦ The **Code**, **Split**, and **Design** buttons in the upper-left corner of the Document toolbar toggle between a code editor, a screen split between a code editor, and a WYSIWYG page, or simply the WYSIWYG view. Most of you will find the **Split** view most effective as it provides quick access to WYSIWYG design tools, plus access to code.

    ◦ The **Live** view when toggled on, displays pages more like they appear in a browser (for example, useful for seeing how links will look in the browser). But you can't edit with the **Live** view toggled on.

    ◦ The **Preview/Debug in Browser** button provides quick previews of your page in any installed browser.

    ◦ The **File Management** buttons allow you to upload the open page directly from the **Design** view without recourse to the **Files** panel.

    ◦ The **WC3 Validation** button accesses tools to test your code.

    ◦ The **Refresh** button updates the **Design** view to match new code.

    ◦ The **Title** field defines the page title that appears in the browsers' title bars.

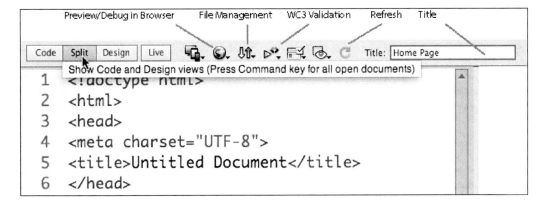

The preceding screenshot illustrates some key tools in the Document toolbar.

4. Choose **File | Save** to save your file. Use lowercase letters and numbers with no spaces or special characters (except _ or -) to ensure your files and links will not get corrupted and will open in the browsers.

    ◦ The **Save As** dialog opens the first time you save a file.

- Use the **Site Root** button in the **Save As** dialog to quickly navigate to your Dreamweaver site's root folder. For smaller sites, you can save all the files directly in this folder. For more complex sites, you can create subfolders within this folder.

- The most widely supported way to define a home page for any folder is to name it `index.html`.

- Use either `.htm` or `.html` for filename extensions, but avoid using both to prevent any chaos that will result from two files with the same name and different extensions.

- When you have entered a valid filename in the **Save As** field, click on **Save**.

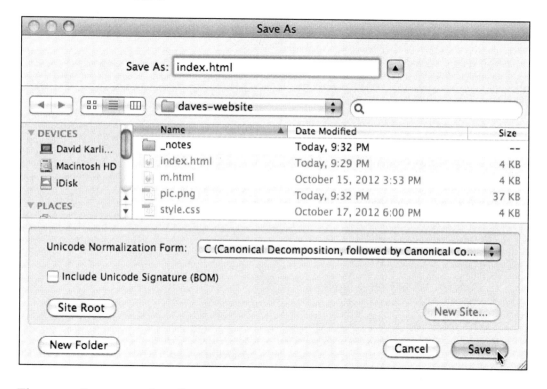

The preceding screenshot illustrates saving an HTML5 page as a home page for a website with the `index.html` filename.

Creating the text content

One of the valuable and productivity-enhancing features in the Dreamweaver Document window is that the **Design** view (or the **Design** side of the **Split** view) serves as a functional word processor. You can compose text here using a standard set of editing tools as you type.

That said, it is more likely you'll copy text content from web pages or word processor documents.

Depending on the source of the text, Dreamweaver offers a set of options for pasting text into the Document window. These are accessed by choosing **Edit | Paste Special**. Use trial-and-error to find the option (ranging from minimalist **Text Only** to options that retain more formatting) that does the best job of pasting copied text into the Document window.

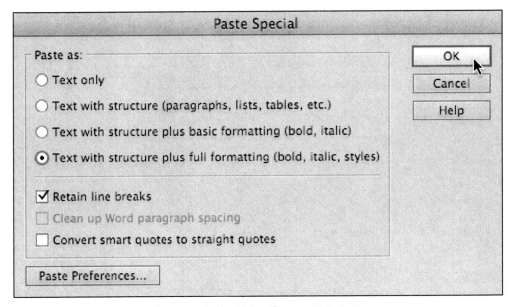

Pasting copied text into a Dreamweaver page

Applying headings

HTML text elements (tags)—headings, paragraphs, and lists—should be used to denote prioritization of content. CSS styles (which we'll soon get to) are used to define how these elements look.

In general, the h1 element is applied to the most important headline(s) on a page, h2 to secondary headlines, and so on.

Apply heading elements by clicking anywhere in a paragraph, and choosing a heading from the **Format** drop-down menu in the **Properties** inspector (if it's not visible, choose **Window | Properties**).

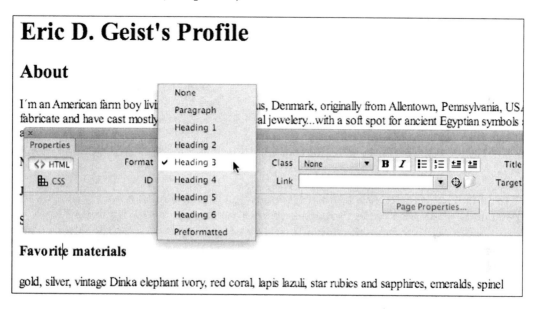

The preceding screenshot illustrates applying an h3 tag to a selected line of text.

Adding paragraphs, lists, and links

By default, the content you enter in the Document window has paragraph tags added to apply paragraph formatting (which includes a line of spacing between paragraphs). You can apply paragraph tags to selected paragraphs from the **Format** drop-down menu in the **Properties** inspector.

Apply ordered (numbered) or unordered (bullet) lists to the selected text by clicking on either of those two icons in the **Properties** inspector.

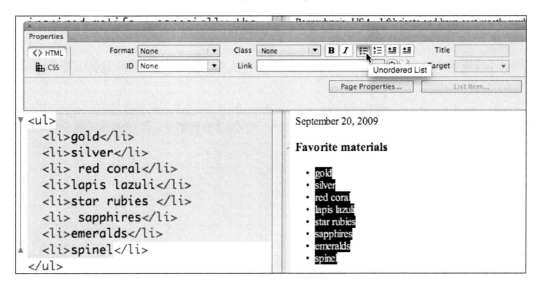

In the preceding screenshot, an unordered list and list tags have been applied in the Document window.

You can assign links to selected text by entering a URL (including the http://www part) in the **Link** field of the **Properties** inspector. Choose _blank from the **Target** drop-down menu to open the link in a new browser window (or tab, depending on the user's configuration). Enter the title text that will display when a link is hovered over in the **Title** field.

In the preceding screenshot, a link is defined that will open in a new browser window; also, a link title is applied.

You can also use the **Browse for File** icon located at the right of the **Link** field, to browse and link to a file in your Dreamweaver site.

Inserting images

If you have your images saved and prepared for the Web, you can embed them by clicking in the Document window to define the insertion point, and choosing **Insert | Image**. The **Select Image Source** dialog appears. Navigate to and select your image file and click on **Open** to insert the image. When you do that, the **Image Tag Accessibility Attributes** dialog appears. Enter text in the **Alternate Text** field that will be accessible to users who have images disabled or are vision impaired. The **Long Description** field can be used to link to HTML pages that describe images when the main audience for your site are users who will not be able to view images.

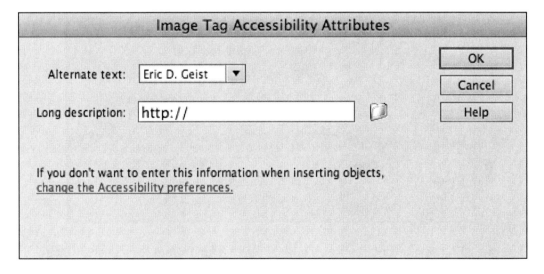

In the preceding screenshot, the alternative text is defined for an image.

You can also copy and paste artwork from any source into the Dreamweaver Document window. Pasting a copied image launches the **Image Optimization** dialog. The **Preset** drop-down menu provides clearly-explained options for converting the image to one of the available web-friendly image formats. Choose one and click on **OK** to insert and launch the **Save Web Image** dialog.

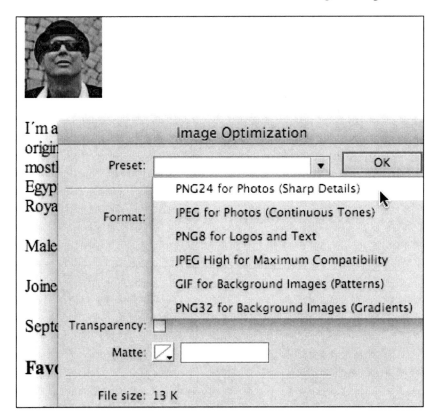

The preceding screenshot illustrates how to select a file format for a pasted image.

In the **Save Web Image** dialog, enter a filename (no spaces or special characters except – or _) in the **Save As** field. Click on **Save** to save the image, as shown in the following screenshot:

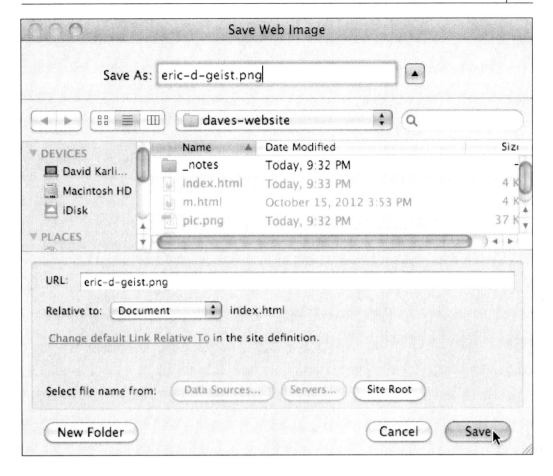

Linking to a stylesheet

Having quickly surveyed the basic techniques required for creating an HTML5 web page with text, images, headings, lists, and links, let's turn to an even more compressed survey of defining and linking that page to an external CSS stylesheet.

External Cascading Style Sheet (CSS) files have been, for some time, the standard way to format web page content, replacing earlier steps in the evolution of web design, such as using data tables for page design, or HTML attributes (for example, `color=red`) for formatting.

We'll return to meshing styles and HTML for designing pages in the next chapter when we structure page content using the new HTML5 elements that are associated with different kinds of content (such as articles, headings, footers, and sidebars). Here, we'll simply establish the basic technique for creating and linking a stylesheet.

Creating and linking to an external stylesheet

A basic website, even a large one, can often function with a single external stylesheet linked to hundreds, even thousands of pages. Keeping styles organized in an external stylesheet allows global updating—when the page background is changed in a stylesheet, the background changes throughout the site.

To create a stylesheet, follow these steps:

1. Choose **File | New** from Dreamweaver's main menu. The **New Document** dialog appears.

2. In the left column, choose **Blank**.

3. In the **Page Type** column, choose **CSS**.

4. Click on **Create**. A new CSS file opens with a `@charset` declaration, which provides support for the widest set of characters, and a comment indicating this is a CSS file.

5. Save the file by choosing **File | Save**. Your stylesheet file can have a simple name such as `style.css` (as always, avoid spaces, upper-cases, or special characters). Enter the filename in the **Save As** field of the **Save As** dialog and click on **Save** to save the file, as shown in the following screenshot:

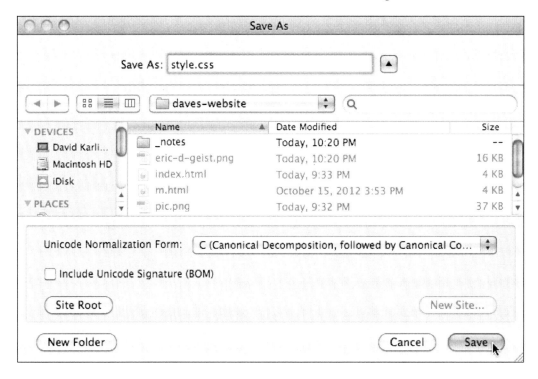

Linking a stylesheet to an HTML file

To link a CSS file to an HTML page, you must first be sure the HTML page is open in the Document window.

Note that after you save the file, you can toggle between your CSS file and your open HTML file(s) in the tabbed bar above the Document toolbar, as shown here (you can toggle between open files using these tabs):

Follow these steps to link a CSS file to an open HTML page:

1. With your HTML file open, view the **CSS Styles** panel (**Window | CSS Styles**).

2. Click on the **Attach Style Sheet** icon at the bottom of the **CSS Styles** panel. The **Attach External Style Sheet** dialog opens.

3. Use the **Browse** button to navigate to and select your CSS file, and click on **OK** in the **Attach External Style Sheet** dialog to link the CSS file to your open HTML page.

4. The linked CSS file now appears in the **CSS Styles** panel (make sure the **All** tab—not the **Current** tab—is selected at the top of the **CSS Styles** panel).

Define the Body tag's style

The single most defining element in any web page is the <body> tag, since it controls all the visible page content. As your stylesheet grows, more specific tags will override the body tag styling, but the style you apply to the body tag sets the default look of your page. So, let's use that as an example for how to define a style in Dreamweaver.

To define a body style with font, font color, and page background color, follow these steps:

1. In the **CSS Styles** panel, click on the **New CSS Rule** icon at the bottom of the panel; the **New CSS Rule** dialog opens.

2. From the **Selector Type** drop-down menu, choose **Tag**.

3. From the **Selector Name** drop-down menu, choose **body**.

4. In the **Rule Definition** drop-down menu, choose your linked stylesheet.

5. Click on **OK** to launch the **Rule Definition** dialog.

6. In the **Type** category, choose a font family from the **Font-family** drop-down menu.

7. Choose other font parameters and values from other drop-down menus and swatches in the **Type** category.

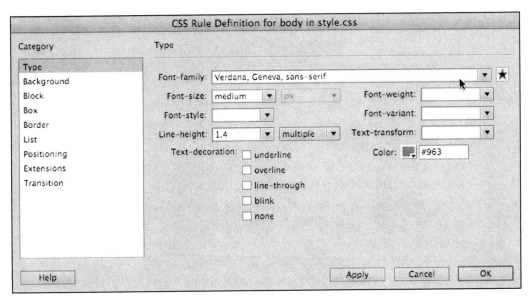

The preceding screenshot illustrates defining a font family for the body element.

8. In the **Background** category of the **CSS Rule Definition...** dialog, choose a background color.

9. Click on **Apply** to preview your settings.

10. Click on **OK** to apply your settings.

Once defined, styles can be tweaked in the bottom half of the **CSS Styles** panel. This is shown in the following screenshot, where the `font-family` property is edited in the **CSS Styles** panel:

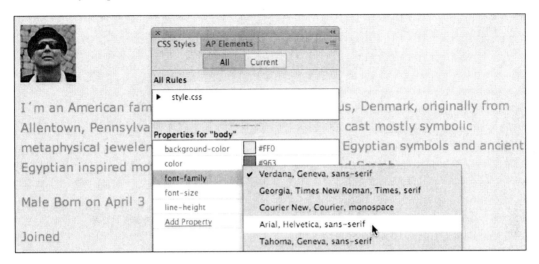

Define a wrapper ID style

Before "wrapping" our compressed exploration/review of basic page building techniques in Dreamweaver CS6, let's apply a "wrapper" `div` tag to constrain our page width and create a separate page background distinct from the page itself.

While the HTML5 styles we create in the following chapter will give us a chance to explore page design with CSS in depth, HTML5 does not come with a "wrapper" element, and we have to create our own.

The technique we apply to do this is to enclose all our page content in a special tag called a **Div** tag. Div tags divide sections of content, and can't do much without having a style associated with them.

Dreamweaver radically streamlines the process of wrapping a page in a wrapper `div` tag. To do that, just follow these steps:

1. With your HTML file open, and your cursor on the **Design** side of the **Split** view, choose **Edit | Select All** to select all the page content.

2. With all the page content selected, choose **Insert | Layout Object | Div tag**. The **Insert Div Tag** dialog opens.

3. Leave the **Insert** drop-down menu set to **Wrap Around the Selection**.

4. Enter `wrapper` in the **ID** field and click on the **New CSS Rule** button. The **New CSS Rule** dialog opens; the following screenshot illustrates how to use the **Insert Div Tag** dialog to create an **ID** style:

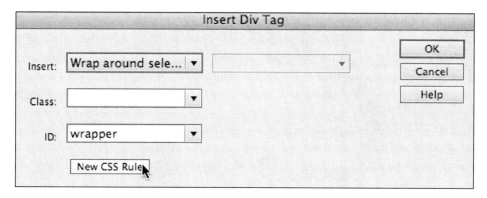

5. In the **New CSS Rule** dialog, simply click on **OK**. The **CSS Rule Definition...** dialog opens.

6. In the **Box** category, enter `950` in the **Width** field to constrain our page width to a standard 960-pixel size (we're going to use up the missing ten pixels with padding).

7. In the **Padding** section of the dialog, enter a value of `5` (px).

8. In the **Margin** section of the dialog, deselect the **Same for All** checkbox and enter `Auto` for the **Left** and **Right** margins to center the wrapper.

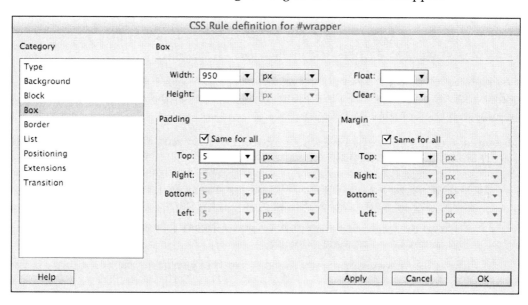

In the preceding screenshot, width, padding, and margin are being defined for an ID style named `wrapper`.

9. In the **Background** category, define a distinct background color for the wrapper (different from the background color for the `body` tag).

10. Click on **OK** to apply the wrapper.

Summary

In this first chapter of the book, we completed a compressed survey of the basic and foundational techniques for working in Dreamweaver CS6. These include defining and working within a Dreamweaver Site, building HTML5 pages, and linking CSS stylesheet files.

We also walked through the process of defining ID `div` tag styles and laying out page content in a container `div` tag. This is the basic building block of modern web page design.

In the next chapter, we'll learn to build web pages in Dreamweaver, relying on HTML5 container tags, which make page content structures more rational and easy to design, and which optimize page content for search engines.

2
Using HTML5 for Page Structure

In the first chapter of this book, we saw a compressed overview of the basic and foundational techniques for working in Dreamweaver CS6: working in a defined Dreamweaver site, building HTML5 pages, linking CSS stylesheet files, and constraining page content in a `<div>` container tag.

In this chapter, we'll learn to build web pages in Dreamweaver using HTML5 container tags. These are the following four things we will accomplish by learning to do that:

- Building page layouts relying exclusively on HTML5 layouts will hone our skills at using these new tools for page design, and introduce HTML5 Code Hints in Dreamweaver

- Relying on *standardized* and *defined* HTML5 layout elements (as opposed to custom-defined, irregularly-implemented div tags) streamlines the page design

- There are actual, significant real-world scenarios where building pages relying exclusively on HTML5 layout elements is the best way to design pages (for example, when designing pages for iPhones or iPads)

- There are functional advantages beyond design considerations for organizing page content in HTML5 layout elements. We will examine those advantages as we build HTML5 pages

In the course of building pages using just HTML5 layout elements, we'll explore all four advantages of relying on HTML5 listed previously.

And here it is important to review, or at least reinforce the following two foundational techniques in building any professional-quality website in Dreamweaver:

1. Do nothing without first defining a Dreamweaver site. Review *Chapter 1, Creating Sites and Pages with Dreamweaver CS6*, if you are not currently working within a defined site.

2. Secondly, and not quite so essential but still pretty foundational: We always work with *external* stylesheets. This allows the styles we define to be applied globally, across an entire website, and makes updating sites possible. As we begin to coordinate styling in the CSS Styles panel and constructing pages with HTML5 elements, I'll be reminding you, and when necessary, walking you through the steps required to make sure all styles are saved to an external stylesheet.

With this as a preview and cautionary reminder, let's dive in to creating pages with HTML5 layout elements.

Structuring pages with HTML5

HTML5 introduced a new approach and opened up new and intuitive techniques for organizing page content. Until the advent of HTML, we had tags that assigned heading levels (H1... H6), paragraph tags, list tags, and other elements that defined mainly how content would be displayed.

When it came to organizing content into containers or boxes, we were left to our own devices. And so developers created their own sets of ID and class styles—ID styles that were used once per HTML file (like a wrapper style), and class styles that were used multiple times on a page (like a style that defined picture/caption boxes).

HTML5 standardizes the elements used to organize content on a page. The key HTML5 structuring elements are as follows:

- `<header>`
- `<nav>`
- `<article>`
- `<section>`
- `<aside>`
- `<footer>`

The names of these elements are pretty much self-explanatory. The `<header>` elements define header content at the top of a page, and `<footer>` elements define footer content. The `<nav>` element defines navigation content. The `<article>` tags define different articles or coherent blocks of content within a page, and larger or longer articles can be subdivided into sections. The `<aside>` elements define sidebar content that should be embedded within an `<article>` or a `<section>` element.

There are other HTML5 elements that define content such as dates, times, and addresses.

Structuring pages with HTML5 elements is referred to as *semantic markup* because these markup elements actually describe the type of content within the tag. Using HTML5 semantic markup accomplishes two things:

- For the developer, HTML5 elements eliminate the need to create a whole set of individually defined `<div>` tag styles.

- For the user, the advantages of HTML5 elements essentially boil down to search engine optimization. By clearly delineating what the content is (a heading, a date, a navigation bar, an article, and so on), HTML5 elements help search engines identify your content and make it accessible.

HTML5 structural elements

Let's continue our exploration of building pages with HTML5 in Dreamweaver CS6. Now, we'll walk through the steps involved in building a fairly complex HTML5 page.

The first step is to alert browsers that we are presenting HTML5 content, for that, we need to indicate at the top of our HTML5 code that this is an HTML5 page. As for those browsers that respond "Huh, what's that?"—I'll explain how to solve that challenge at the end of this chapter. But first, use the following steps to create a new HTML5 page from scratch:

1. With your Dreamweaver site defined, choose **File | New**. In the **New Document** dialog, choose **Blank Page** from the category list on the left-hand side of the dialog. Choose **HTML** in the **Page Type** column. Choose **<none>** in the **Layout** column.

2. The **Layout CSS** pop up is set to **Create New File**. Remember, we'll be saving our styles to an external stylesheet. If you already have a CSS file to use with HTML layouts, you could choose **Link to Exiting File** instead, and select your existing HTML5-related CSS file as the styles file for your page.

3. From the **DocType** pop up, choose **HTML 5** if that is not already selected, as shown in the following screenshot:

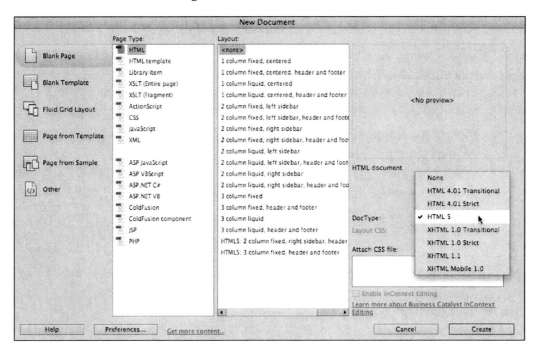

The preceding screenshot shows a new HTML5 page being generated in the **New Document** dialog.

4. Click on **Create** to generate the blank page.

A blank page appears in the **Design** view of the **Document** window. In the **Split** view, we can see that the following basic code has been generated:

```
<!doctype html>
<html>
<head>
<meta charset="UTF-8">
<title>Untitled Document</title>
</head>
<body>

</body>
</html>
```

Breaking down HTML5 page code

Let's quickly walk through this basic code to situate ourselves.

The `<!DOCTYPE HTML>` and `<html>` tags are sort of evolutionary holdovers from previous versions of HTML, and not actually required for HTML5 browsers. This code might be useful when taking into account non-HTML5 browsers, as we will be examining shortly. By the way, the `<!DOCTYPE>` declaration for HTML5 is not case sensitive.

And here's another intriguing thing about an HTML5 `<!DOCTYPE>` declarations. By telling browsers that we are structuring our content in HTML5, we are also telling older browsers to be less strict in enforcing rules, such as ending every paragraph element with `</p>`. Thus, we avoid annoying and unnecessary browser error messages.

Back to our generated code:

The `<head>` and `</head>` tags demarcate the head content that is not displayed on the page, but serves as instructions to browsers.

In this case, the content inside the `<head>` element identifies that the current, most widely applicable character set, **UTF-8**, is implemented. This character set allows the display of characters from a wide range of languages.

All of the content we create for the page will be placed within the `<body>` and `</body>` tags. For this reason, our first step in creating our CSS styles for this page, will be to define a couple of basic attributes for the `</body>` tag.

Finally, save this page as an HTML file. Choose **File | Save**. In the **Save As** dialog, make sure the folder selected in the **Where** pop up is your Dreamweaver site folder (or a subfolder within that). Give the file a name, such as html5_test, and click on **Save**.

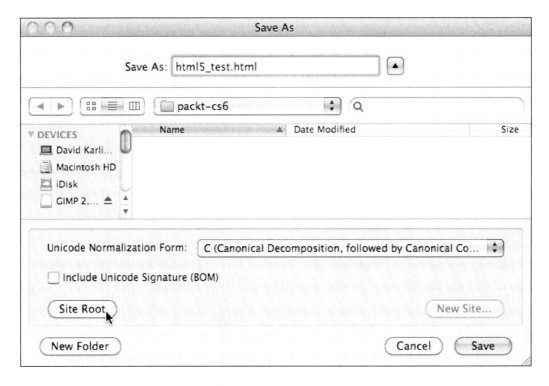

The preceding screenshot shows how to save an HTML5 page.

While we're at it, enter a descriptive title in the **Title** box of the **Document** toolbar. Re-save periodically.

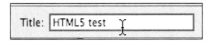

The preceding screenshot shows how to define a page title.

Using HTML5 structure elements

Having set up our HTML5 document with basic web page coding, we're now ready to create and format the HTML5 layout elements that will define how the page looks.

A basic HTML5 page layout is illustrated in the following screenshot. It demonstrates a certain hierarchy to the page. All content is constrained (for size) within a traditional wrapper `div` tag. Within that, the page has a header, a footer, and `article` elements. The `section` elements are present within `article` elements.

Note also that the `nav` element (holding navigation content) can be used either inside another element (such as a header or footer) or outside any HTML5 semantic layout elements. And, note that an `aside` element can be used within either an `article` or a `section` element.

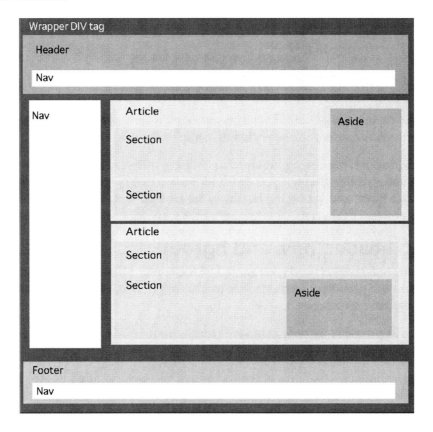

The preceding screenshot shows an HTML5 page layout.

Using Code Hints

I won't mince words, Dreamweaver CS6 pretty much eschews any WYSIWYG support for HTML5 page structuring. At this stage of the game, most of us use Dreamweaver's **Split** view anyway, and Dreamweaver's **Code** view (available as half the screen in the **Split** view) has helpful code-hinting for creating HTML5 page structure. As you begin typing HTML5 elements in the **Code** view, beginning with <, Dreamweaver prompts you with a set of tags that begin with the letter you type. So, for example, typing <he produces code hints from which you can click on **<>header** and press the *Enter* key (Windows) or the *Return* key (Mac) to place the code.

Dreamweaver provides code hinting for HTML5 semantic layout elements, as shown in the following screenshot:

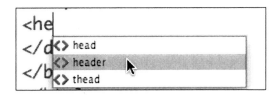

To *close* (define the end of) an HTML5 layout element, simply type </. When you do that, Dreamweaver auto-enters the closing code for the open element.

As we walk through the coding involved in defining different HTML5 layout elements in the remainder of this chapter, you can enter the necessary code in the **Split** view, utilizing code hints, and seeing the results in the **Design** view of the **Split** view.

Adding header, nav, and hgroup

The <header> element is used to organize all the content that goes at the top of a page. Within the <header> element, you might well include the <nav> content as shown in the next screenshot.

And, you will probably include standard (traditional) HTML tags such as headings and links.

So, the <nav> content—the links at the top of a page—are included in the <header> element when they are placed at the top of a page. Navigation elements placed in sidebars are also enclosed with the <nav> element, but since—in this case—they are not part of the header, they are not enclosed in the <header> element.

Within a <header> element, CSS styles associated with tags (<h1>, <h2>, and so on), or with the class <div> tags can be used to supply additional formatting rules for how content will be displayed.

With the aim of making content within a header more easily categorized, HTML5 includes the `<hgroup>` element. The formal requirement for the `<hgroup>` content is that it should include at least one heading tag (`<h1>`, `<h2>`, `<h3>`, `<h4>`, `<h5>`, or `<h6>`).

The concept is that the heading content such as subheadings, alternative titles, or taglines should all be grouped within a header for easy access. So, for example, in the next screenshot, the two heading lines have been wrapped in an `<hgroup>` element. But the navigation content, although part of the header, is not included in the `<hgroup>` element.

In the following code, an `<h1>` heading and an `<h2>` heading, along with a `<nav>` element with its own `<h5>` heading (and three placeholder links), are all part of a `<header>` element:

```
<header>
<hgroup>
<h1>Page header</h1>
<h2>Header 2 </h2>
</hgroup>
<nav><h5>Navigate: <a href="#">link 1</a> | <a href="#">link 2</a> |
<a href="#">link 3</a></h5>

</nav>
</header>
```

The following screenshot illustrates how this looks in the **Split** view in Dreamweaver (with the **Live** view on in the **Design** view side of **Split** view).

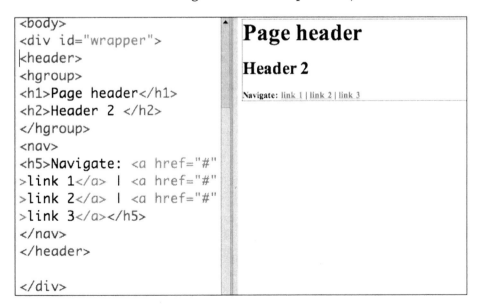

Creating articles and sections

If you write for a living, like I do, you learn to organize content into chunks and sub-chunks, concepts and sub-concepts, ideas and more detailed ideas, and so on. The basic rule for organizing content in this way is that if you create a sub-section, you have to create two subsections. Otherwise, there's no point in creating just one subsection.

In line with our recurring theme of unity between content and design in HTML5 layout, the content in HTML5 pages, where it has to be broken down, is broken down into what are called **articles**. And, where there is a need for distinct subsections within an article, those subsections are **sections**.

As you create a CSS file to match your HTML layout elements, you might well assign specific formatting to articles and to sections. For example, you might choose to indent section content or place a unique background behind it.

The code for the `<article>` and `<section>` elements in the preceding illustration, including the placeholder text and headings is as follows:

```
<article>
<h3>First article</h3>

<p>First article content ....</p>

<p>more content....</p>

<section>

<h3>1st section heading</h3>
<p>1st section content</p>
</section>

<section>
<h3>2nd section heading</h3>

<p>2nd section content</p></section>

</article>
```

Or, you might choose *not* to apply specific CSS rules to articles and sections, and simply wrap the content in the `<article>` and `<section>` elements for content-organizing purposes while relying on the `<body>` tag, the `<p>` (paragraph) tag, or custom class styles that you define in Dreamweaver for formatting the article and section content.

Adding aside content

Aside is reserved for sidebar content that is dependent on the content present in an article or section of an article. The `<aside>` element is not intended, for example, to serve as a container for navigation content (navigation content is supposed to be identified by and wrapped in the `<nav>` element discussed earlier).

Given that aside content is generally formatted as a sidebar, there is a particular style generally associated with the use of `<aside>` elements: Float. The CSS Float attribute moves a container to the left-hand side (`float:left`) or to the right-hand side (`float:right`) of other content, and flows other content around the container. When we'll define CSS styles for our HTML5 semantic layout elements at the end of this chapter, we'll be sure to float our `<aside>` element style.

Creating a footer

The final piece of an HTML5 page layout is usually a `<footer>` element. As with all HTML5 layout elements, `<footer>` elements have content assignments. Footers usually include site content author information, legal notices (such as copyright information), and so on.

An HTML5 layout template

The following code incorporates all the HTML5 semantic layout elements discussed so far. Feel free to copy and paste it into the **Code** side of Dreamweaver's **Split** view and use it to experiment with and familiarize yourself with HTML5 page structuring.

And, this code will provide a good basis to experiment with CSS styling for HTML5 elements—the next step in our journey:

```
<!doctype html>
<html>
<head>
<meta charset="UTF-8">
<title>HTML5 test</title>
<link href="html5_layout.css" rel="stylesheet" type="text/css">
</head>
<body>
<div id="wrapper">
<header>
<hgroup>
<h1>Page header</h1>
<h2>Header 2 </h2>
</hgroup>
```

```
<nav>
<h5>Navigate: <a href="#">link 1</a> | <a href="#">link 2</a> | <a
href="#">link 3</a></h5>
</nav>
</header>
<article>
<h3>First article</h3>
<p>First article content ....</p>
<p>more content....</p>
<section>
<h3>1st section heading</h3>
<aside>
<p>Sidebar content</p>
<figure>
<p><img src="http://upload.wikimedia.org/wikipedia/commons/6/63/
Wikipedia-logo.png" height="150" width="150"></p>
<figcaption>Caption </figcaption>
</figure>
</aside>
<p>1st section content</p>
</section>
<section>
<h3>2nd section heading</h3>
<p>2nd section content</p>
</section>
<h3>Second article</h3>
<p>Second article content ....</p>
<p>more content....</p>
<section>
<h3>1st section heading</h3>
<p>1st section content</p>
</section>
<section>
<h3>2nd section heading</h3>
<p>2nd section content</p>
</section>
</article>
<footer>
<h5>Footer content </h5>
<address>Contact us at <a href="http://www.website.us" target="_
blank">www.website.us</a>
</address>
</footer>
</div>
</body>
</html>
```

This code example includes one metadata element that we haven't explored yet—a `<figure>` element. I figured I'd throw it into the code so as to keep things organized and simple, but let's now move on to exploring this and other HTML5 metadata elements.

Adding metadata

The HTML5 layout elements we've explored thus far have—as we have seen—a dual function: They serve as styleable elements that can control how content is displayed, and they organize content for accessibility. These HTML5 elements can be thought of as metadata.

Both the style and content dimensions of HTML5 layout elements are evolving, but already they serve as tools for designing pages and for delivering content. The example we explored earlier of being able to easily select an article or an article section for copying on an iPhone gives a taste of how this is likely to evolve in the near future.

In addition to the key layout elements explored so far, it is worth briefly noting a few HTML5 elements whose main role it is to index content (even though they can be used to apply styles as well).

Defining an address

Often, one of the first things a visitor to a site seeks is, contact information such as a URL (if the page is not a site's home page), an e-mail address, or a physical address if he or she is looking to locate the hottest underground club or the nearest highly-rated shish-kabob stand.

An `<address>` element can be placed within any other HTML5 semantic layout element such as an `<article>` element if it is providing contact information for the author of (or topic of) the article. Or, an `<address>` element can be associated with (placed within) a `<footer>` element if it is providing contact information for the entire page.

Figures and captions

The `<figure>` and `<figcaption>` elements identify a figure, and an associated caption intuitively enough. Again, assigning these elements to content helps content aggregators and indexing programs (such as search engines) interpret your page content and make it more accessible. And, you can use these elements to style figures and/or captions as well.

For example, a `<figure>` element can be wrapped around both an image and a caption (`<figcaption>`).

Indicating date and time

Speaking of using HTML5 elements to convey content, there are different HTML5 elements associated with different kinds of time and date information.

The `<time>` element is used to mark off times and dates for upcoming events. It is not intended to define every reference to a date and time. You would not, for example, use the `<time>` element when citing dates for different historical events while writing an historical article.

The `<time>` element can be used to set off a specific time, as in the following HTML5 code:

```
The show starts at <time>12:00</time>.
```

Or, date and time information can be encoded within text using the `datetime` parameter, as shown in the following line of code:

```
<time datetime="2012-01-01">all night jam session!</time>
```

The format for time and date is: `YYYY-MM-DDThh:mm:ssTZD`, where `TZD` is the time zone.

You are unlikely to use the `<time>` element as a styling tool. Instead, it is best used to demarcate dates and times.

Creating a CSS file for HTML5 page structure

Hand-in-hand with our HTML5 file, designers create and use a CSS file to organize and manage all the styling in the page. So, let's create that CSS file now, and as we do, add a line that will make our HTML5 page compatible with all current browsers and most older ones.

To do that, perform the following steps:

1. Navigate to **File** | **New**, and in the **New Document** dialog, choose the **Blank Page** category on the left-hand side, and **CSS** from the **Page Type** category. Click on **Create** to generate and open a new CSS file.

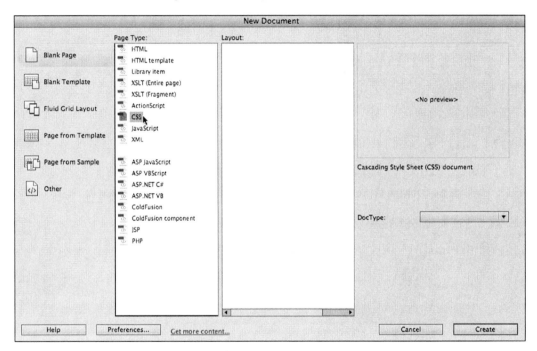

The preceding screenshot shows the generation of a new CSS file.

2. The file opens in **Code** view. We'll be editing it in the **CSS Styles** panel, so—except as a learning experience—we won't need to view this page again. But we do need to save it. Navigate to **File | Save**, and give the file a name such as `html5_layout.css`. Make sure the site folder is selected in the **Where** pop up, and click on **Save**, as shown in the following screenshot:

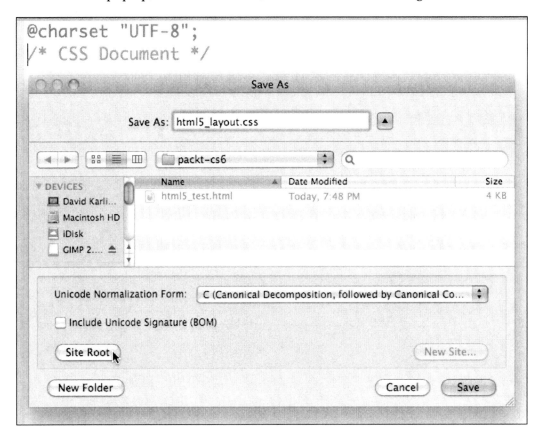

The preceding screenshot displays saving a CSS file.

3. In the tab bar at the top of the document window, toggle back to the HTML file you created.

4. View the **CSS Styles** panel (if it is not visible, navigate to **Window | CSS Styles**), and click on the **Attach Style Sheet** icon as shown in the following screenshot:

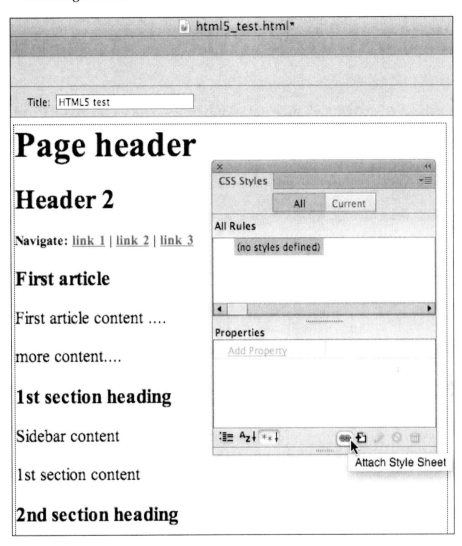

5. The **Attach External Style Sheet** dialog appears. Use the **Browse** button to navigate to the CSS file you just created, and click on **OK** to attach the stylesheet. The CSS file appears in the **CSS Files** panel (use the **All** tab in the **CSS Styles** panel as the norm, unless you are doing some detective work on particular styles, which may require the **Current** tab). You will also see the link to the CSS file in the **Code** view.

Assigning a block property

Next, we will add a single attribute that enables most browsers to interpret the HTML5 elements even if they are not HTML5 compliant. Here, we'll be revisiting the technique we noted in the previous chapter where we saw how Dreamweaver CS6's HTML5 layouts use the `display:block` CSS attribute to keep HTML5 layouts from collapsing in non-HTML5 browsers.

To do that, perform the following steps:

1. Click on the **New CSS Rule** icon at the bottom of the **CSS Styles** panel—it is just to the right-hand side of the **Attach Style Sheet** icon identified in the previous figure. The **New CSS Rule** dialog appears.

2. In the **New CSS Rule** dialog, choose **Compound** from the first pop up. We are creating a rule that will apply to more than one HTML5 layout element. These are HTML5 tags that we want to prevent from collapsing when viewed in non-HTML5 browsers.

3. In the **Choose or Enter a Name for Your Selector** field, enter `header`. We actually want to apply the rule we're working on to additional HTML5 elements, but we'll add those shortly. In the **Rule Definition** section of the dialog, make sure your attached CSS file is selected (it will be by default). Click on **OK**.

4. In the **CSS Rule Definition for Header** dialog, select the **Block** category, choose **Block** from the **Display** pop up as shown in the following screenshot, and then click on **OK**:

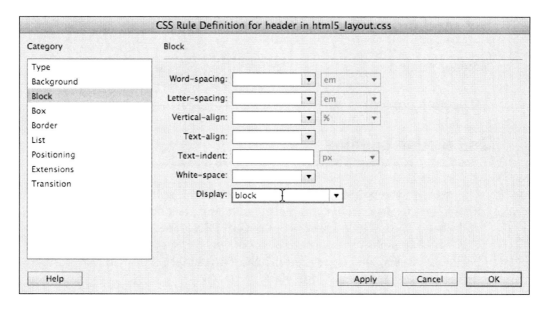

The preceding screenshot displays the process of defining a block display.

5. The `header` style appears in the **CSS Styles** panel when you expand the CSS styles file linked to the page. You can see that the **display** property for the header style has a **block** attribute associated with it in the **CSS Styles** panel.

6. We want to expand the list of HTML5 elements to which this `display:block` attribute is assigned. The long, slow way to do that is to duplicate steps we've traversed so far for each additional element. To do that the quick and easy way, click once in the header row in the top half of the **CSS Styles** panel, and edit the list of elements to include the `<address>`, `<article>`, `<footer>`, `<nav>`, and `<section>` elements. Use commas (",") to separate the additional elements as you type them in. These are HTML5 tags that we want to prevent from collapsing when viewed in non-HTML5 browsers. The **CSS Styles** panel should now look like the the following screenshot:

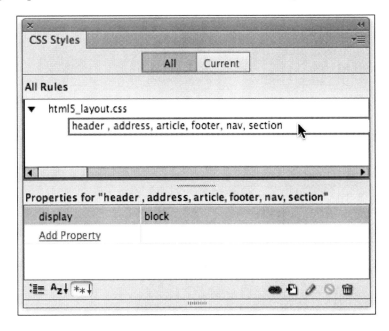

The preceding screenshot shows the process of assigning a block display to multiple HTML5 semantic layout tags.

With the preceding set of steps, we've told most non-HTML5 browsers to keep our basic HTML5 building-block elements on their own distinct horizontal row, so they don't get smushed into each other.

Defining styles

I won't bore you here by rehearsing the basic techniques for defining styles within a linked stylesheet in Dreamweaver CS6. We walked through this in a compressed way, for review, in *Chapter 1, Creating Sites and Pages with Dreamweaver CS6*, and we defined one (compound) style in our linked CSS file in the previous set of steps.

To quickly review, new CSS style definitions are added to the linked stylesheet by clicking on the **New CSS Rule** icon at the bottom of the **CSS Styles** panel. All the styles we'll create are tag-type styles, applying as they do to HTML5 semantic elements (tags).

You can define the following styles in that manner using the **CSS Styles** panel. Or, you can enter (or copy) the following code into your CSS stylesheet after the compound style we just created:

```
@charset "UTF-8";
/* CSS Document */
header , address, article, footer, nav, section{
  display: block;
}
header {

color: #FFF;
  background-color: #CCC;
}
footer {
  color: #000;
  background-color: #FFF;
}
article {
  color: #000;
}
aside {
  float: right;
  width: 200px;
  border: thin solid #FFF;
  background-color: #999;
  padding: 10px;
  margin: 10px;
}
figure {
  background-color: #CCC;
  margin: 10px;
  padding: 10px;
```

```
    float: right;
    width: 160px;
    height: 180px;
}
section {
    padding: 0px;
}
```

 A few notes on the CSS we created: We're using very minimalist background and text colors (shades of gray plus white and black) both to make a minimalist aesthetic statement and to keep our project simple.

The `float` attribute on the `<aside>` element aligns the aside (sidebar) box with the right-hand side of the page, flowing content around it to the right-hand side. The extra padding and margin enforce spacing both, between the aside content and the border of the box, and between the box itself and the content that flows around it.

Similarly, the `float` and `margin` attributes assigned to the `<figure>` element align the box that will hold images and captions with the right-hand side of the page.

Setting the `margin` to zero for the article sections keeps that content from indenting further beyond the indent inherited from the margin assigned to the `<article>` and `<section>` elements.

Solving HTML5 compatibility challenges

At the time of writing this book, HTML5 is a work in progress. What does that mean? In historic terms, it means the standards for HTML5 are still being systematized, although a critical mass has been reached where the meaning and effect of most HTML5 terms is widely agreed upon, and browsers either support HTML5, or they are evolving in that direction in finite terms.

For developers, it means that as we explore the time- and stress-saving features of HTML5 to build web pages, we have to be aware of, and compensate for the fact that some browsers will not support some aspects of HTML5.

In the main, that means supporting the stubbornly-entrenched Internet Explorer community, particularly older versions of IE whose users have been abandoned by Microsoft, which does not provide upgrade options for most of those users.

In order to not leave these users locked out of HTML5 pages, developers have adopted the HTML5 Shiv script and the designer's link to it. That JavaScript allows IE8 to recognize HTML5 semantic structure tags.

To add the HTML5 Shiv JavaScript to pages, insert the following code in the `<head>` element of your page:

```
<!--[if lt IE 9]><script src="http://html5shiv.googlecode.com/svn/
trunk/html5.js"></script><![endif]-->
```

Summary

In this chapter, we explored using HTML5 semantic layout elements to build pages in Dreamweaver. We saw how these elements function as both design containers, and as content identifiers. We also saw how, for some environments, an entire page can be built using only a few basic HTML tags plus HTML layout elements.

In the next chapter, we will explore Dreamweaver CS6's powerful tools for generating validated forms.

3
Collecting Data with Forms

In the Facebook-dominated world of the modern web, data collection has become highly opaque. When you share an intimate thought about a dying friend over social media, that sensitive, personal data becomes a commodity that is sold to marketers of flowers and books on death, when you *Like* a band in a social media environment, you (often unwittingly) sign up to get offers for tickets when that band is playing near your city or town, and so on.

I am being harsh on the opacity of online "sign up" technology to make a point. As someone building your own site, you can instead, make the collection of data voluntary, conscious, and transparent. People who sign up, on purpose, for your e-newsletter, your announcements, your special offers, and so on are—after all—likely to be more receptive to getting mail from you than the ones they did not consciously ask for, but that were generated by their activity on Facebook, Amazon, and so on.

So how do you collect information from visitors? One word: **forms**. Forms can be a vital, dynamic way of interacting with your visitors.

The following are some examples of how forms lend value to your site:

- A feedback form that lets visitors to your site share their complaints, suggestions, and positive experiences (fodder for you to use to promote your site, message, product, cause, or content).
- A sign up form that lets visitors consciously get your newsletter, tweets, special offers, and information blasts.
- An order form to sell products.
- A search box that makes your site's content easily accessible. I'll show you how to set one up at the end of this chapter.

Dreamweaver CS6 has powerful tools for building inviting, accessible forms. What I have always found missing in Dreamweaver is a way to connect those forms to backend server tools that handle submitted data. And while a full exploration of those connections is a bit beyond the scope of this book, I'll provide some basic solutions and tips for additional tools and resources that can be used for connecting forms to backend data-management scripts and resources at the end of this chapter.

Capturing client-side form management with JavaScript

Dreamweaver generates forms, but it doesn't manage form data. In general, data collected from a form is sent to a server where a collection of scripts and databases turn that data into a processed order, a submitted complaint, an e-mail list signup, or a search query. Scripts that handle data on a server are sometimes called **server-side scripts**.

But some form data is collected and managed without being sent to a server. Instead, submitted data is managed using JavaScript that runs in a user's browser. Data handled by such client-side scripting never goes to a server.

The most widely used client-side form is a **jump menu**—a dropdown menu used for navigation. Dreamweaver allows you to easily generate a jump menu, and before launching into an exploration of building forms that send data to a server, let's take a quick look at how to build a client-side jump menu in Dreamweaver, and edit the generated JavaScript that makes that form work.

Creating a jump menu

Before you create a jump menu, you'll want to have a list of URLs you want to access with that menu. I'll pause for a moment while you collect your list...Ok? Well, this is a book, so you can simply bookmark this spot (easy to do on your Kindle or iPad, but if you're reading a printed book, simply bend the page a bit to mark this spot).

Beyond conceptualizing your jump menu, you need to have the following in place before generating the menu:

- You need to be working in a defined Dreamweaver site. If that's not ringing a bell, go back to *Chapter 1, Creating Sites and Pages with Dreamweaver CS6*, and immerse yourself in the concept of a Dreamweaver site and why it's the essential first step in everything you do in Dreamweaver.

- You need to be working in a saved web page.

Working in a Dreamweaver site and in a saved HTML5 page will ensure that whatever links you generate in your jump menu will work.

With your list ready, your site defined, and your page saved, perform the following steps to create a jump menu in Dreamweaver CS6:

1. With your insertion point in the **Design** view of a page, choose **Insert | Form | Jump Menu**. The **Insert Jump Menu** dialog opens.

2. The dialog opens with the first menu item selected. Often, the first item in a jump menu is not an option, but a label that identifies the menu, such as **Go to...**. In that case, the **When selected go to URL** field is left blank, as shown in the following screenshot:

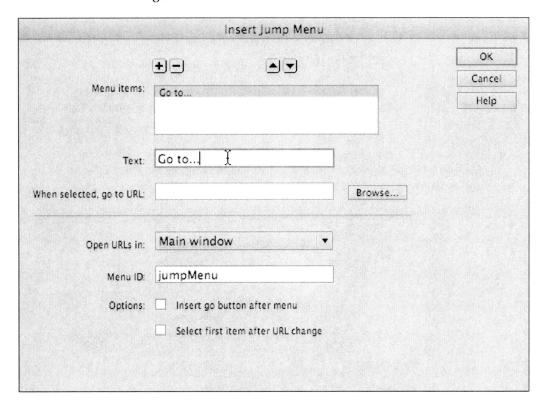

3. Use the **Add Item** (+) icon to add items to the menu. Use the **Browse...** button to search for and add link to files in your Dreamweaver site. Or, enter a full URL in the **When selected, go to URL** field, as shown in the following screenshot:

4. Use the **Add Item** (+) icon to add additional items to the menu. Use the **Remove Item** (-) icon to delete a selected item, as shown in the following screenshot:

5. Use the **Move item up in list** and **Move item down in list** arrow buttons to resort the order of your list (should you alphabetize?), as shown in the following screenshot:

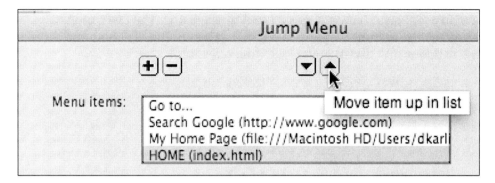

6. When you finish defining your jump menu, click on **OK** to generate the menu. You can test the menu in the **Live** view as shown in the following screenshot:

Editing Jump Menu JavaScript

Dreamweaver provides two ways to edit the content of a generated jump menu—the **Properties** inspector, and the **Behaviors** panel. Let's quickly see how each of these works.

To activate the **Properties** inspector, navigate to **Window | Properties** if it is not visible. When you click on any element (including a jump menu) the **Properties** inspector becomes a context-sensitive editing tool. In this case, the **Initially Selected** dropdown menu allows you to change what option in the menu displays by default, and the **List Values...** button opens a **List Values** dialog. The **List Values** dialog has tools you recognize from the jump menu dialog for adding, deleting, and reordering the menu options, as shown in the following screenshot:

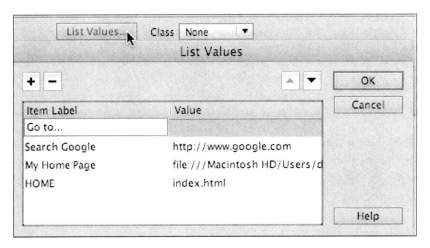

The other technique for editing the content of a jump menu is a bit less accessible, but provides the option of using the **Browse** button to locate and link to files in your Dreamweaver site. To access that option, choose **Window | Behaviors**, and click on your jump menu in the **Design** view of the **Document** window as shown in the following screenshot:

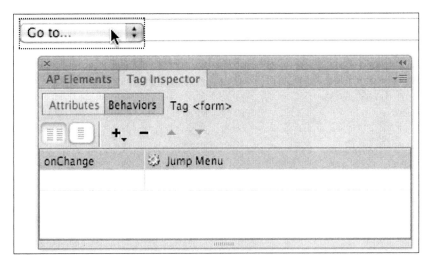

With the jump menu selected in the **Behaviors** panel (technically, the **Behaviors** tab in the **Tag Inspector** tab), double-click on **Jump Menu** in the right-hand side column to (re)open the **Jump Menu** dialog. This option enables full-featured editing on your jump menu — pretty much duplicating the original **Jump Menu** dialog.

Having quickly looked at JavaScript-based forms, and how to edit them in Dreamweaver, let's move to the more powerful kind of form — one that sends data to a server.

Defining the form and form action

Forms are comprised of a form and form elements. The **form element** is the envelope in which all the form elements are gathered up and sent somewhere. As such, the most important defining element of the form is the form action. The **form action** defines where the form data is sent.

As alluded to earlier in this chapter, Dreamweaver designs the frontend for forms, but does not provide easily-accessible options for linking that form data to a backend system that collects and manages that data.

Note that Adobe offers a package for managing server-side data — **Business Catalyst**. Business Catalyst's tools and features are not particularly accessible for non-professional backend administrators, and for most freelance and small-scale developers, the cost of this service is not competitive with other options for managing form data.

At the end of this chapter, I'll provide some basic techniques for capturing form data, and point you towards other resources. But here, let's use the simplest and most basic technique for handling form data: Sending that form data to an e-mail address through a user's e-mail client. This is not an elegant technique, but a) it works, and can be used for simpler form handling challenges such as collecting feedback; and b) it will serve as kind of a placeholder for form handling until we return to the concept at the end of this chapter.

To insert a form that sends collected content to an e-mail address using a user's e-mail client, perform the following steps:

1. Click on the **Design** view of an open, saved document to set the insertion where the form will appear.

2. Navigate to **Insert | Form | Form**.

3. Click on **OK** to embed the form. The form appears in the **Design** view in a red box. When you select the form (by clicking on the red box), the **Properties** inspector displays the form properties, as shown in the following screenshot:

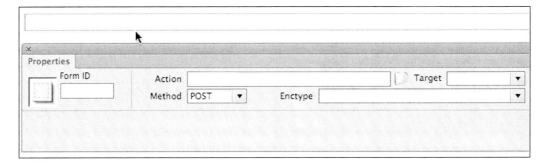

4. To send the form data to an e-mail address, enter `mailto:mail@mail.com` in the **Action** field, substituting a real e-mail address for the placeholder e-mail address.

5. In the **Enctype** field (short for encoding type) enter `text/plain`.

6. Leave the **Method** option set to the default, **POST**. This is how most form data is sent.

With the form defined, you are now ready to add form fields and buttons.

Generating form fields with Spry validation

Validation means testing form data before it is submitted to a server (or sent to an e-mail address). That's a valuable thing. For example, if your form is collecting e-mail addresses for e-newsletter subscriptions, it won't do for people to submit the form without an e-mail address. Beyond that, validation can look at the characters entered into an e-mail address field and verify that what is in the field at least looks like an e-mail address.

There are essentially three techniques for validating form data as follows:

- Server-side scripts can validate content once it is sent to the server
- HTML5 provides some validation tools, but they are not yet supported universally, even in newer versions of some popular browsers
- JavaScript validation scripts can test data in a browser

The last option is the most reliable, fastest, and easiest way to create in Dreamweaver. And in the following sets of steps, we'll use Dreamweaver's library of Spry JavaScript and HTML to insert fields with built-in JavaScript validation.

Creating a validated text field

Text fields are the bread and butter of forms, collecting all manner of text, such as names, phone numbers, account numbers, addresses, and e-mail addresses (more on those shortly).

 At the risk of sounding awfully redundant, let me re-emphasize the importance of creating validated fields in a defined Dreamweaver site and in a saved HTML file. This takes on special importance now, because we are generating JavaScript files that will be linked to our page, and if those links are corrupted, the form won't work.

The most common type of validation for a text field is to make it *required*. Perform the following steps to insert a required text field in a form:

1. Navigate to **Insert | Form | Spry Validation Text Field**. The **Input Tag Accessibility Attributes** dialog appears.

2. The **ID** field generates an ID style associated with the form field. This attribute is used in some environments to make forms more accessible for people with disabilities and also allows you to define an ID style that applies to the form field. Enter an ID style with no spaces or special characters.

3. The **Label** field generates a label that identifies the field and is easily read by software that aids disabled web users. Enter a label (the label can have special characters and spaces) as shown in the following screenshot. The other fields in the dialog can be left at their default settings, so click on **OK**, as shown in the following screenshot, to generate the form:

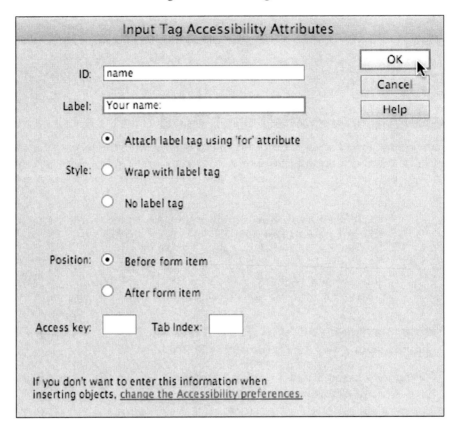

4. Form field attributes can be defined by clicking on the form field itself in the **Design** view and making edits in the **Properties** inspector. Enter a value in the **Char width** field to define how wide the field will display (in characters). Enter a value in the **Max chars** field to define the maximum number of characters a user can enter in the field, as shown in the following screenshot:

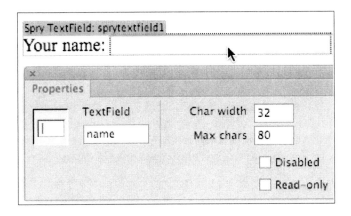

5. Validation rules are defined by clicking on the (aqua colored) **Spry TextField** tab above the field itself. By default, our **name** field is required. You can add validation rules by entering a maximum or minimum number of characters in the **Max chars** or **Min chars** fields. And, by default, the field is validated on Submit—when a user submits the form. You can also force validation when a user leaves the field by checking the **Blur** and **Change** checkboxes (these two options accomplish similar things in different browsing environments).

6. You can preview how the field will respond to valid or invalid entries by experimenting with options in the **Preview states** dropdown list. The area below the preview shows the result if a user attempts to submit the form without filling in a required field, as shown here:

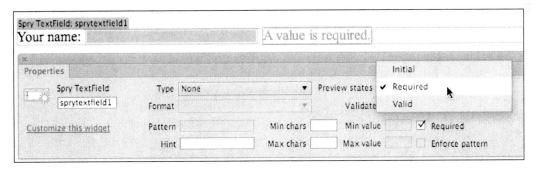

7. After you define the field and the validation rules, click to place your insertion point at the end of the form field in the **Design** view, and press the *Enter* or *Return* key to create a new line for a new form field.

Creating a validated e-mail field

Creating a validated e-mail field is similar to creating a text field, except that you'll set the validation rules to detect (and only accept) input that looks like an e-mail address.

To do that, click on the (aqua) **Spry TextField** tab for an e-mail address form field, and select **Email Address** from the **Type** dropdown menu in the **Properties** inspector. And, select the **Enforce Pattern** checkbox on the right-hand side of the **Properties** inspector, as shown in the following screenshot:

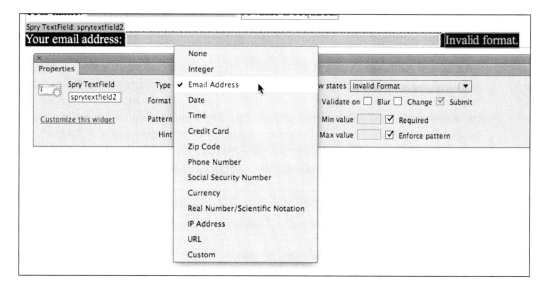

As you can see from looking at the options in the **Type** dropdown list, Dreamweaver can generate a whole range of validation scripts for different kinds of text input, ranging from phone numbers to credit cards.

Adding other fields

The submenus in **Insert | Form** includes options for generating additional types of validated form fields. The most important of these are as follows:

- **Checkbox**: Used for *yes or no* choices, where a user can select or deselect an option.
- **Select**: Used to create dropdown menus with options within a form.
- **Radio Group**: Used to create sets of options from which a user can chose only one. For example, to allow a user to choose one (and only one) type of credit card.

These additional validated form fields are pretty self-explanatory with the background we covered in discussing options for text fields. They are illustrated in the following screenshot (from top to bottom: checkbox, select menu, and radio group):

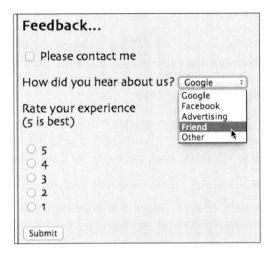

Adding Submit and Reset buttons

Without a **Submit** button, the content a user enters into the form literally doesn't go anywhere. A **Submit** button in a form launches the form action. So, if we apply the rules of formal logic here, we better make sure our form has a **Submit** button.

Add a **Submit** button by navigating to **Insert | Form | Button**. The **Input Tag Accessibility Attributes** dialog box appears, but just click on **OK** to create the **Submit** button without worrying about the options in this dialog box. A **Submit** button appears on your form.

Reset buttons are handy, but not essential. They "reset" the form to its original (empty) state. To create a **Reset** button, insert a second button. With that button selected in the form, choose the **Reset Form** radio button in the **Properties** inspector, as shown in the following screenshot:

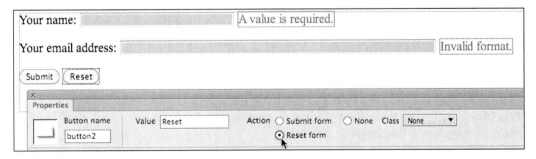

Prompting with HTML5

As noted earlier in this chapter, browser support for HTML5 form elements and properties is a work in progress. For that reason, I'd advise against using HTML5 form attributes that are *essential* for the form to work—such as validation attributes.

But HTML5 placeholders are a good idea. They prompt a user with text inside the form field that disappears as a user enters content. If the user's environment doesn't support HTML5 form placeholders, they can still rely on the form label to help them figure out what to enter into the form field.

A placeholder parameter can be added to a text input. Unfortunately, Dreamweaver CS6 doesn't offer options for defining placeholder text in the **Design** view, but we can do this in the **Code** view. To do that, perform the following steps:

1. Select the **Split** view from Dreamweaver's **Document** window.

2. Click on a form field in the **Design** side of the **Split** view to find the code on the **Code** side of the **Split** view, as shown on the following screenshot:

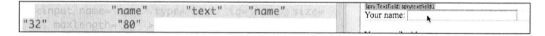

3. At the end of the input tag, add placeholder="placeholder text" (replace "placeholder text" with real text), as shown in the following screenshot:

```
<input name="name" type="text"
id="name" size="32" maxlength="80"
placeholder="Type your full name
here">
```

You can preview placeholder text in the **Live** view, in the **Design** side of the **Split** view.

Designing CSS for forms

In the first two chapters of this book, we established a framework of relying on external CSS stylesheet files to provide formatting for HTML elements (such as headings, paragraphs, and links) and special ID and class styles that can be applied to the div tags to design pages.

How does that doctrine apply to customizing form input? The short answer is: You create styles for the different form elements. The long answer: Well, we'll walk through how to do that now.

The following are the key HTML elements to which CSS styles can be applied to customize form appearance:

- The `<form>` element style defines the appearance of the entire form.
- The `<input>` element style defines the appearance of input fields (such as text fields).
- Specific ID styles can be defined for styles that have IDs associated with them (a technique we examined earlier in this chapter when I showed you how to assign an ID to a text field in the **Input Tag Accessibility Attributes** dialog (see the *Creating a validated text field* section).

Creating a stylesheet for form elements

Let's walk through the process of defining each of these styles in a new, linked CSS file. We'll name it as `form.css`.

1. As always, starting from a saved HTML page in a defined Dreamweaver site, view the **CSS Styles** panel (**Window | CSS Styles**). Click on the **New CSS Rule (+)** icon at the bottom of the panel, as shown in the following screenshot:

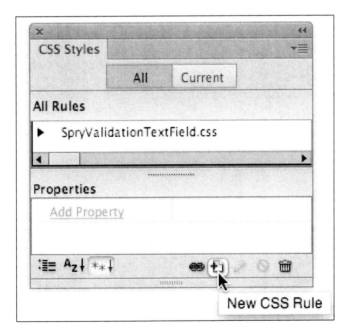

Note that if you are working with a form that includes Spry validation widgets, your **CSS Styles** panel will be linked to a CSS file that defines elements of those widgets that style things such as background colors and fonts for validation error messages.

2. In the **New CSS Selector Rule** dialog, choose the following:
    - **Tag** from the **Selector Type** dropdown list
    - **form** from the **Selector Name** dropdown list
    - **(New Style Sheet File)** from the **Rule Definition** dropdown list

3. Click on **OK** to begin defining the new file and style, as shown in the following screenshot:

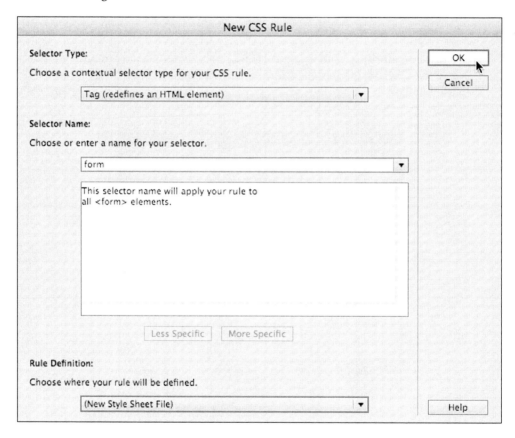

4. In the **Save Style Sheet File As** dialog, click on the **Site Root** button to save your file in your Dreamweaver site's root folder. In the **Save As** field, enter `form.css`. Click on **Save**. The **CSS Rule Definition** dialog appears.

5. You might want to define a background color for your form style. Do that in the **Background** category of the **CSS Rule Definition** dialog (choose a color from the **Background-color** swatch).

6. You can also define a width for your form to constrain it from stretching the entire width of the page (or enclosing element). Do that by entering a width (such as 600 px) in the **Width** field of the **Box** category. Also, in the **Box** category, try defining 10 px of padding and a 10 px margin for the form.

7. Try defining a border for your form. At any time you can click on the **Apply** button on the **CSS Rule Definition** dialog to test your styling, as shown in the following screenshot:

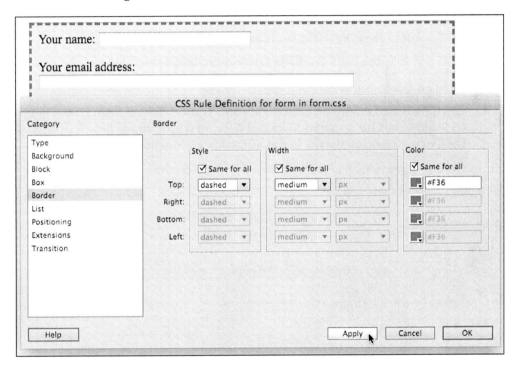

8. After you fine-tune your form style, click on **OK** in the **CSS Rule Definition** dialog to save and apply your style.

9. Navigate to **File | Save All** to save both your web page and the CSS file with changes.

Creating styles for form elements

In the same way that you defined a style for the `<form>` element, you can create a new style for the `<input>` element. The only difference is that once you've created a CSS file for forms (`form.css`), you will want to save all form-related styles to that CSS file. I'll get you started with the following steps:

1. Switch to the **Live** view in the **Document** window for a more accurate preview of the style you are about to define.

2. Click on the **New CSS Rule** (+) icon at the bottom of the panel. The **New CSS Selector Rule** dialog opens, choose the following:
   - ° **Tag** from the **Selector Type** dropdown list
   - ° **Input** from the **Selector Name** dropdown list
   - ° `form.css` from the **Rule Definition** dropdown list

3. Click on **OK** to begin defining the new style.

4. The **CSS Rule Definition** dialog appears. You can take it from here — define style attributes for an input field and click on **Apply** to see how they look in the **Design** view, as shown in the following screenshot:

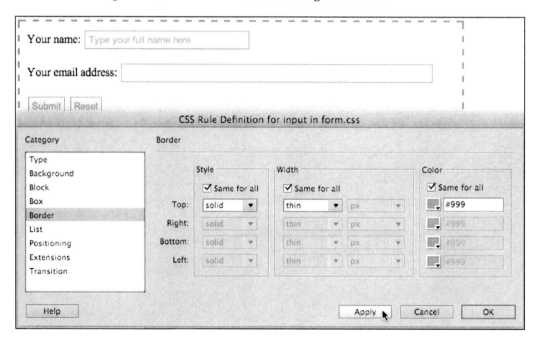

5. Click on **OK** when you have defined the style for input fields.

Creating ID styles for a form

So far, the styles we've created apply to every instance of an element. For example, our form style attributes (background color, width, and so on) will apply to every form. And our input style attributes apply to every input element (name and e-mail fields and submit and reset buttons).

How do you define a style that applies only to a specific element? One technique is to use the IDs associated with the fields we created when we generated Spry validation fields.

Perform the following steps to use an ID style for one of the ID elements we generated as we created fields:

1. Click on the **New CSS Rule (+)** icon at the bottom of the panel. The **New CSS Selector Rule** dialog opens, choose the following:

    ◦ **ID** from the **Selector Type** dropdown list

    ◦ **name** from the **Selector Name** dropdown list

    ◦ **form.css** from the **Rule Definition** dropdown list

2. Click on **OK** to open the **CSS Rule Definition** dialog.

3. Define custom styling for the **name** ID element, testing your style by clicking on **Apply**, as shown in the following screenshot:

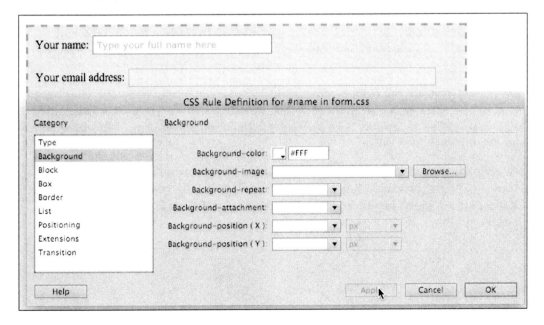

4. Click on **OK** to define the style for the **name** ID element.

5. Navigate to **File | Save All** to save changes to your HTML and CSS files.

Thoughts on form styles

In the framework in which we are exploring forms here, we are working with a form we designed ourselves. In "real life", particularly in more sophisticated professional projects, the HTML for a form will be supplied by the team that builds the backend scripts and databases that manage the form input.

But I want to emphasize that you can still create CSS files and styles that customize the look of those forms. So, the form HTML you get from Google for a search engine, the form HTML you get from www.TheSiteWizard.com to manage feedback, and the form HTML you get from an e-commerce add-in package, can all be customized with your own CSS. And in that way, forms can be integrated into the inviting look and feel you craft for your site.

Real-world form handling

While I've emphasized that Adobe does not provide an accessible, reasonably-priced framework for managing form data, there are tons of online resources, many of them free, that plug into Dreamweaver sites easily. Before closing this chapter, I want to walk you through an example of a **FreeFind box**.

I picked that example because rare is the site that doesn't use a search box, and also because installing (and customizing) a Freefind search box is free and pretty straightforward.

For this to work, all you need is a live website hosted at a remote server. Getting set up with one of those is a bit more complex. Refer back to the *Defining a remote site* section in *Chapter 1, Creating Sites and Pages with Dreamweaver CS6*, of this book for advice on how to do that.

The following set of steps draw on techniques covered earlier in this chapter, so if you're bouncing directly to this point in the book to install a search box, you're best off jumping up to the beginning of the chapter first for form and form style basics.

So, with that proviso, perform the following steps to add a search box to your site:

1. Navigate to **File | New** and create a new page that will hold your search box by performing the following steps:

    1. In the left-hand side column of the **New Document** dialog, choose **Blank Page**.

    2. In the **Page Type** column choose **HTML**.

    3. In the **Layout** column choose **<none>**.

    4. Click on **Create** to generate the new page.

    5. In the **Title** area of the **Document** toolbar, type Search this site

    6. Save the page in the root folder of your site as search.html.

    7. Use the **Attach Style Sheet** icon in the **CSS Styles** panel to link the form.css style to this page. You'll be using the same set of styles you created for a signup form earlier in this chapter.

2. In a browser, go to www.freefind.com. To sign up for a search box, perform the following steps:

    1. Enter your name, e-mail, and click on the **Instant Sign-up** button. You'll get login information sent to your e-mail address.

    2. Use the login information sent to your e-mail address to log in to your FreeFind account. The sign-in process will take you directly to the **Control** window for your search box.

    3. FreeFind offers reasonably priced ad-free options, but you can use the free version to experiment with forms and styles, so there is no need to subscribe to any special plans.

    4. Click on the **HTML** tab in the **Control** window, as shown in the following screenshot:

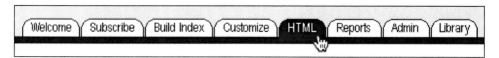

3. To copy and paste the HTML for the search box, perform the following steps:

    1. To keep things simple, we will use the first option for a search box, **1. Site search box - with a link to advanced search options**.

2. Click on the link beneath that option that says **get the html and paste it into your page**. The HTML is displayed in a box as shown in the following screenshot:

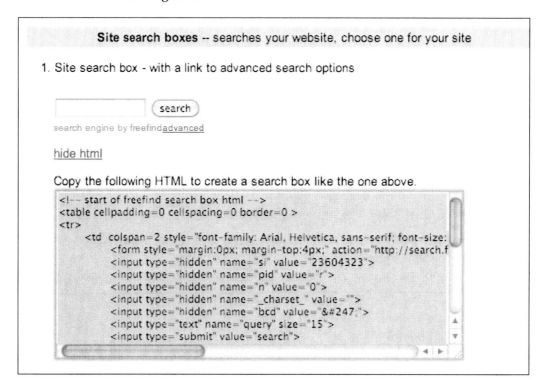

3. Click inside the code, and copy it to your clipboard.

4. Switch back to your open Dreamweaver HTML file (`search.html`). In the **Code** side of the **Split** view, click to place your insertion point after the end of the `<body>` tag and press the *Enter* or *Return* key to create a new line of code.

5. Paste the copied HTML from FreeFind, and view the result in **Live** view in the **Design** side of the **Split** view as shown in the following screenshot:

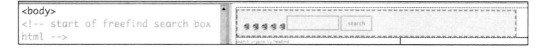

6. The FreeFind code is cluttered with table formatting. You can remove that code in the **Code** side of the **Split** view if you wish, or just accept it. But more importantly, you can use the **Properties** inspector and other editing techniques we've explored in this book so far to customize the form. I'll let you review this chapter as both a practical application of what we've covered, and something of a "test" to strengthen your confidence and skill at formatting forms to accomplish the following:

   ○ Change the width of the search field to 48 characters, and the maximum characters to 60

   ○ Add this placeholder text: `search string goes here`

   ○ Add a Reset button

   ○ As long as you don't change the form field names or delete them (including the hidden form fields that will not display in a browser but will allow FreeFind's search box to function), you can edit both the HTML and CSS for your form, as shown in the following screenshot (in **Live** view):

   ○ By using your `form.css` stylesheet, you'll make the FreeFind search box look and feel like other forms in your site.

The FreeFind example was simpler than some forms you'll get from third parties. But the basic technique of generating HTML for a form, pasting that form into Dreamweaver, editing the form HTML (without deleting or renaming any form fields), and applying your own custom styling... well that works with any form you get from anywhere.

Summary

In this chapter, we explored Dreamweaver CS6's powerful tools for generating validated forms. To do that, we invoked the Spry framework—a set of widgets that combine HTML, CSS, and JavaScript to apply different kinds of interactivity to web pages. We will be revisiting the set of Spry widgets in Dreamweaver CS6 several times in later chapters in this book.

We also learned to create a simple jump menu with Dreamweaver-generated JavaScript. So, from a couple of different directions, we began to explore Dreamweaver's JavaScript features in relation to forms.

Then, we went beyond what Dreamweaver does with forms—specifically adding a placeholder attribute to fields with prompt text. We had to go into the **Code** view to do that as Dreamweaver's support for new HTML5 attributes is paltry.

And finally, you worked through a real-life example of connecting a form with a backend system of scripts and databases. The FreeFind search example was relatively simple, but it had all the elements you'll need to handle in order to embed a form supplied by any backend server into a Dreamweaver CS6 site. And in relation to this, I want to highlight the dynamic role of custom CSS in making the embedded form look and feel like the rest of our site. We'll return to CSS formatting in substantially more depth in the next chapter.

4
Applying CSS3 Effects and Transforms

CSS3—the current version of stylesheets—provides easy access to effects, such as drop shadows, rounded box corners, and opacity (transparency). Additionally, CSS3 introduces transforms that change the shape, location, rotation, and size of objects. Together, CSS3 effects and transforms open the door to making web pages more dynamic, more inviting, less "boxy", and more interactive.

Effects and transforms can be made interactive by changing the appearance of objects as a user hovers over or clicks on them with a mouse. Together, effects and transforms, with or without animation, make it much easier than the previous tools to add accessible, inviting design elements and dynamism to web pages.

CSS3 effects and transforms are defined through stylesheets; so, we can take advantage of Dreamweaver's **CSS Styles** panel to avoid much, if any, recourse to handcoding, to create them.

In this chapter we will explore the following:

- Defining and applying CSS3 transforms: translate, scale, rotate, and skew
- Defining and applying CSS3 effects: border radius, shadows, and opacity
- Combining multiple transforms and effects
- Making CSS3 transforms and effects interactive with `:hover` pseudo-classes

New in CSS3–effects and transforms

CSS3 effects, such as shadows, rounded corners, and opacity, can make web pages more stylish, less harsh, and more welcoming. When used with discretion (that is, not overused), they make web pages attractive and inviting.

Effects and transforms can be, and often should be, combined to produce eye-catching elements. The following text, for example, has both a skew transform and a shadow (box-shadow) effect applied:

Lorem ipsum dolor sit amet, consectetur adipiscing elit. Phasellus nec lacus tellus. Aenean ac euismod lectus. Aliquam ac tristique est. Etiam mattis pretium libero eget tristique. Phasellus convallis dignissim tellus, nec consectetur dui molestie ornare. Nam neque justo, mollis quis suscipit vitae, consectetur nec lacus.

Aenean commodo, nunc vitae pretium dictum, nulla augue dictum lorem, in scelerisque sapien neque ut felis. Sed sit amet dui eget libero consequat aliquet. Proin libero leo, adipiscing eget adipiscing ut, pretium sit amet dolor.

Vestibulum ultricies feugiat hendrerit. Mauris varius tincidunt tellus, a euismod mi vehicula lobortis. Aenean ante libero, aliquam vitae ultrices eget, venenatis sit amet nibh. In hac habitasse platea dictumst. Mauris auctor, ante ac gravida interdum, dui arcu malesuada ligula, sit amet congue elit arcu at ante. Fusce convallis egestas adipiscing. Donec ullamcorper adipiscing convallis. Aenean eget blandit libero. Nulla a odio sed nibh luctus tincidunt. Etiam tempor enim in ligula pellentesque congue.

Transitions, such as skewing, rotating, scaling, and translation (moving) objects, are particularly engaging when combined with interactivity. For example, a visitor to a website who hovers over an object experiences a subtle but inviting change in it.

In the pre-CSS3 era, these kinds of effects or transitions required some combination coding and embedding Flash objects by relying on (and programming with) JavaScript and substituting images with Photoshop effects for types (for features such as shadows or outlining). These other tools were (are!) expensive and/or have a high learning curve.

During the course of this chapter, we'll explore several new effects and the new 2D (two-dimensional) transforms in CSS3. 3D transforms are beyond the scope of our survey; they are not as widely supported in browsing environments and, generally, additional scripting (usually JavaScript) is required to make them effective.

The bulk of this chapter will consist of walking through how to create particular CSS3 effects and transforms.

Compatibility challenges

CSS3 effects and transitions are widely supported without the need for plugins (such as JavaScript or Flash).

On the other hand, it is important to emphasize that HTML5 and CSS3 features are all a work in progress. In searching for a formulation to describe the state of support for CSS3 in browsers, I bumped into the formulation, **irregular standardization**. I realize that it's an oxymoron, but what I mean is that the CSS3 effects and transforms we are creating in this chapter are supported in the current versions of all the major browsers (and yes, that includes Internet Explorer 9 along with Safari for mobile and desktop; Firefox and Opera).

However, Safari, Firefox, and Opera all require unique code prefixes. For example, the CSS3 code for a class style to apply the `rotate` transform to rotate a box five degrees counterclockwise might look like the following:

```
rotate {

  transform: rotate(-5deg);

  -webkit-transform:rotate(-5deg);

  moz-transform:rotate(-5deg);
  o-transform:rotate(-5deg);
}
```

The `-webkit-` prefix applies to Safari and other browsers that adhere to the WebKit standard (which, by the way, includes Dreamweaver CS6's **Live** view). The `-moz-` prefix applies to Mozilla Firefox. The `-o-` prefix applies to the Opera browser. And the generic transform code applies to "everyone else" including Internet Explorer 9 that does not require a browser prefix to interpret this (or other) effects.

The lack of standardized coding is not as big a problem as it might seem. It just requires a bit of redundancy as we define and apply effects and transforms.

What about browsing environments, such as the older versions of Internet Explorer, that do not support CSS3 effects and transforms at all? There is an easy and a hard answer to that challenge. The hard solution is to patch together JavaScript and other coding solutions that can be found online or that have been concocted to simulate the effects and transforms not supported in CSS3. Which is to say, you can revert to tools and techniques such as JavaScript and Flash that were required to produce these effects before the advent of CSS3.

The easier, and probably more sensible, solution in most cases is to employ transforms and effects in ways that do not require that a browser supports the effect in order for a visitor to absorb page content. For example, have a look at a rounded rectangle created using the `border-radius` effect in the following screenshot:

Lorem ipsum dolor sit amet, consectetur adipiscing elit. Phasellus nec lacus tellus. Aenean ac euismod lectus. Aliquam ac tristique est. Etiam mattis pretium libero eget tristique. Phasellus convallis dignissim tellus, nec consectetur dui molestie ornare. Nam neque justo, mollis quis suscipit vitae, consectetur nec lacus.

Aenean commodo, nunc vitae pretium dictum, nulla augue dictum lorem, in scelerisque sapien neque ut felis. Sed sit amet dui eget libero consequat aliquet. Proin libero leo, adipiscing eget adipiscing ut, pretium sit amet dolor. Vestibulum ultricies feugiat hendrerit. Mauris varius tincidunt tellus, a euismod mi vehicula lobortis. Aenean ante libero, aliquam vitae ultrices eget, venenatis sit amet nibh. In hac habitasse platea dictumst. Mauris auctor, ante ac gravida interdum, dui arcu malesuada ligula, sit amet congue elit arcu at ante. Fusce convallis egestas adipiscing. Donec ullamcorper adipiscing convallis. Aenean eget blandit libero. Nulla a odio sed nibh luctus tincidunt. Etiam tempor enim in ligula pellentesque congue.

If someone visits the page in the preceding example using an older version of Internet Explorer, such as IE6, they will forgo the experience of seeing the type in a circle (defined by the `border-radius` effect). Not quite as inviting an experience, but they will still be able to read the text as shown in the following screenshot:

Lorem ipsum dolor sit amet, consectetur adipiscing elit. Phasellus nec lacus tellus. Aenean ac euismod lectus. Aliquam ac tristique est. Etiam mattis pretium libero eget tristique. Phasellus convallis dignissim tellus, nec consectetur dui molestie ornare. Nam neque justo, mollis quis suscipit vitae, consectetur nec lacus.

Aenean commodo, nunc vitae pretium dictum, nulla augue dictum lorem, in scelerisque sapien neque ut felis. Sed sit amet dui eget libero consequat aliquet. Proin libero leo, adipiscing eget adipiscing ut, pretium sit amet dolor. Vestibulum ultricies feugiat hendrerit. Mauris varius tincidunt tellus, a euismod mi vehicula lobortis. Aenean ante libero, aliquam vitae ultrices eget, venenatis sit amet nibh. In hac habitasse platea dictumst. Mauris auctor, ante ac gravida interdum, dui arcu malesuada ligula, sit amet congue elit arcu at ante. Fusce convallis egestas adipiscing. Donec ullamcorper adipiscing convallis. Aenean eget blandit libero. Nulla a odio sed nibh luctus tincidunt. Etiam tempor enim in ligula pellentesque congue.

Before diving into *how* to apply transforms and effects, let's reflect for a moment on the advantages involved with using these CSS3 features to format the examples we've previewed so far. No Flash or JavaScript was created, injured, mistreated, or worse while creating these effects. All that was required was a few lines of CSS that we generate in Dreamweaver's **CSS Styles** panel.

Nor was it necessary to use "image text", the type saved as an image, to create these effects. The page can load almost instantly, without waiting for an image to download. In the absence of plugins or images, the shaping and formatting gets downloaded more or less instantly, without browsers having to mess with plugins or downloaded images.

And, finally, the text is still *selectable*. This means that the text to which transforms or effects have been applied can still be copied and pasted into a map program, a calendar event, or selected as a text link as shown in the following screenshot:

CSS3 styles in Dreamweaver CS6

Dreamweaver CS6 provides some features for defining and applying these new CSS3 features. While not the most powerful tools in Dreamweaver, they do make it possible to create and apply new CSS3 techniques without resorting to coding. Where coding is essential, Dreamweaver helps out with code hints.

There are essentially two options for getting our money's worth out of Dreamweaver as we generate CSS3 transforms and effects:

- If we enter the CSS code in the **Code** view, Dreamweaver will help with the coding by supplying code hints. For example, the following screenshot shows a code hint being offered after `-moz-tran` has been entered in the **Code** view. Code hints for the stylesheet provide easy access to the `transform-` attribute.

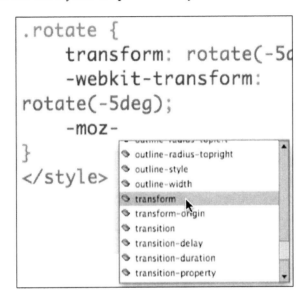

Redundant CSS code

The preceding screenshot shows what is a big part of an ongoing dimension of defining and applying CSS3 transforms and effects. You have to create four versions of the code, one for Webkit (Safari), one for Mozilla (Firefox), one for Opera (a browser with a large user base in Europe), and a generic version (with no browser prefix) that is recognized by Internet Explorer 9. We'll return to this challenge in this chapter shortly.

- The other option is to generate CSS3 effects and transforms in the **CSS Styles** panel. The downside to this is that these new CSS3 style rules do not show up in the **CSS Rule Definition** dialog, which is normally the most user friendly and intuitive environment for defining CSS styles in Dreamweaver.

You *can*, however, enter CSS3 effects and transforms through the **Add Property** link at the bottom of the **CSS Styles** panel. And Dreamweaver CS6 (or older versions with the HTML5 Pack installed) *will* generate CSS code based on the style rules and parameters you enter in the **CSS Styles** panel. With this option, Dreamweaver will at least "bust" you if you attempt to enter an invalid CSS3 rule, as shown in the following screenshot (in the following example, I should be entering `-moz-transform` and then defining the **skew** transform in the right-hand side column of the **CSS Styles** panel).

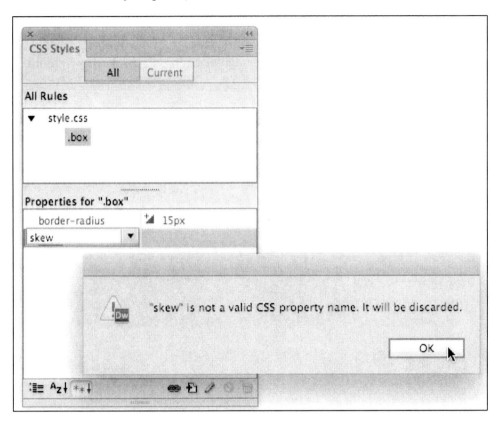

Let us speak bluntly for a moment. Neither of these options—relying on code hints in the **Code** view or using Dreamweaver's **CSS Styles** panel—is really up to the level of assistance we get from Dreamweaver CS6 when we generate pre-CSS3 styles. The folks at Adobe, we presume, are scrambling like everyone else to catch up with current and emerging web design tools.

I'll leave it to you to decide which of these useful but flawed techniques to use for defining CSS3 effects and styles, and I'll illustrate both techniques in the remainder of this chapter.

CSS3 effects

As noted already, support for CSS3 effects and transforms is irregular and a work in progress. Within that framework, the four available transforms (scale, translate, rotate, and skew) are relatively stable and widely supported. Effects, on the other hand, are less consistently supported and less finite in the sense of there being a "list" of available effects that are supported (albeit with unique coding prefixes) across browsing environments.

Part of the reason for this is that a number of effects are very flexible. For example, the text-shadow effect can be tweaked to produce an outlined type. And sometimes, you will hear people refer to an "outline" effect, by which they mean adjusting the parameters of the text-shadow effect to create an outlined type as shown in the following screenshot:

With what has been discussed so far about the flexible and open-ended nature of CSS3 effects, let's examine three of the most useful effects: opacity, border radius, and shadow (for both boxes and text).

Defining opacity

The `opacity` effect in CSS3 allows you to apply varying degrees of opacity/ transparency to objects. The syntax is as follows:

```
opacity:x;
```

In the preceding syntax, x is a value between zero and one. Full opacity (a value of 1) is normal—the object to which opacity is applied acts like a cover over everything else. Full transparency (a value of 0) makes an object invisible. An opacity value of .6 makes an object 60 percent opaque, and so on.

In spite of all the preceding warnings that CSS3 effects have to be defined specifically for different browsers, the `opacity` effect is one that does *not* require a prefix for identifying target browsers.

Simple or complicated

With CSS3, implementing opacity (transparency) is quite simple, or rather hopelessly complex, depending on what one is aiming for. Using opacity to create a complex set of layered objects with various elements having their own assigned opacity requires complex coding and is not supported by all browsers.

Opacity can be applied to a tag (conceivably, for example, the `<img>` tag that defines how images appear). Of more efficacy is the technique of defining a class style that applies opacity. You can do that with the following steps:

1. In the **CSS Styles** panel, click on the **New CSS Rule** icon at the bottom of the panel to launch the **New CSS Rule** dialog. Choose **Class** from the **Selector Type** pop-up menu, enter a name (no spaces or special characters— **semi_opaque** would work), and select your external stylesheet from the **Rule Definition** pop up. Click on **OK**.

2. The **CSS Rule Definition** dialog opens. Sadly, as discussed earlier, CSS3 effects cannot be defined in the **CSS Rule Definition** dialog. So, simply click on **OK** to create a new CSS rule without properties at this stage. The new rule, however, will appear in the **CSS Styles** panel, which is where we will define the opacity settings.

3. With your newly created class style selected in the **CSS Styles** panel, click on the **Add Property** link in the bottom-half of the **CSS Styles** panel. In the first column type `opacity`, and press the *Tab* key to move to the second column. In the second column, type a value between 0 (for complete transparency) and 1 (for full opacity). The value `.5`, for example, defines 50 percent transparency as shown in the following screenshot:

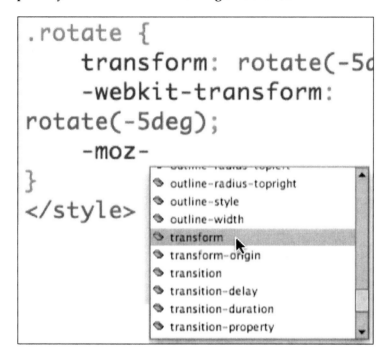

With the class style defined, you can apply it to selected objects (such as an image) by choosing the class style from the **Properties** inspector.

After you define a CSS class style, you can apply it to any selected element from the **Class** drop-down menu in the **Properties** inspector as shown in the following screenshot:

You can test opacity effects in different browsers. While opacity is not supported in all browsers—particularly older versions of browsers—its application is usually such that if it works, it can enhance a page, but if it doesn't work, no essential content is lost. The following screenshot shows text on top of an image. The text on the left-hand side is displayed with full opacity. The text on the right-hand side is displayed with partial transparency, allowing visitors to see some page background behind the text.

Border radius

The CSS3 `border-radius` effect is used to define rounded corners.

Let's dive right into an example of a class style that applies rounded corners with a 12-pixel radius to a 150-pixel square box, and a yellow background with a thick, solid red line around it. In the previous discussion of creating a class style to apply opacity effects, we used the technique of building the class style in the **CSS Styles** panel. That worked well because opacity effects are pretty simple. Here, let's build the style in a CSS stylesheet. Assuming you have an external stylesheet linked to an open web page in Dreamweaver, you can add this code to the CSS file to define a `border-radius` class style:

```
.box {

  background-color: yellow;

  height: 150px;

  width: 150px;

  border: thick solid red;

  -webkit-border-radius: 12px;

  -moz-border-radius: 12px;

  border-radius: 12px;

}
```

The code we're working with here uses the `-moz-` prefix to support Firefox. The following screenshot shows this class style applied to a selected text in Dreamweaver:

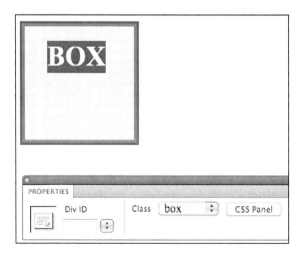

In a browser, the preceding image looks like the following screenshot:

One fun technique to try is to create a circle affected by making the rounded-radius value equal to half the height (and width) of a square box. The following example shows the effect, with the values adjusted from the earlier example so that the rounded radius is 75 pixels, half the pixels that define the dimensions of the original square.

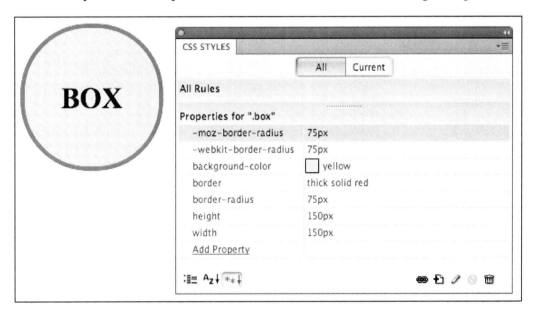

Shadows

Drop shadows may well be the most widely applied effect in graphic design. Don't quote me on that, but shadows certainly are a ubiquitous element in many designs; and now, they're easy to apply to selected objects using CSS3.

There are two different shadow effects: box-shadow and text-shadow. Their application is pretty self-explanatory; box-shadow applies to boxes and text-shadow to text.

Both `box-shadow` and `text-shadow` effects can be defined with a minimum of two parameters: x-offset (vertical distance) and y-offset (horizontal distance). In addition to this, they usually include a color (if no color is specified, a browser-default color appears) and a blur parameter (the thickness of the blur gradient).

x and y offset values can be positive or negative. Positive values generate a shadow on the right-hand side of the text while negative values generate a shadow on the left-hand side of the text. For the y-offset values, positive values generate a shadow below the text while negative values create a shadow above the text. Values are normally defined in pixels.

Before examining how this works for boxes, text, and outlines, it is useful to note that *multiple* shadow definitions can be combined. So, for example, if you wish to generate a shadow under *and* over the text (and you will want to do this when you define an outline style), you can combine two or even three shadow definitions, and they are stacked on top of each other.

Box shadow

As noted, `box-shadow` effects are usually defined with four parameters: offset-x (horizontal distance), offset-y (vertical distance), blur (width in pixels), and the color of the shadow.

The following code, for example, defines a box shadow with 5 pixels of horizontal and vertical offset, a blur length of 5 pixels, and a gray shadow — and it does so for five different browsers, namely Chrome, Safari, Firefox, (using the unprefixed code) Internet Explorer 9, and Opera.

```
.shadow {

  -webkit-box-shadow: 5px 5px 5px gray;

  -moz-box-shadow: 5px 5px 5px gray;


  box-shadow: 5px 5px 5px gray;
}
```

Here's how that looks in the **CSS Styles** panel (and you could define the class style in the **CSS Styles** panel).

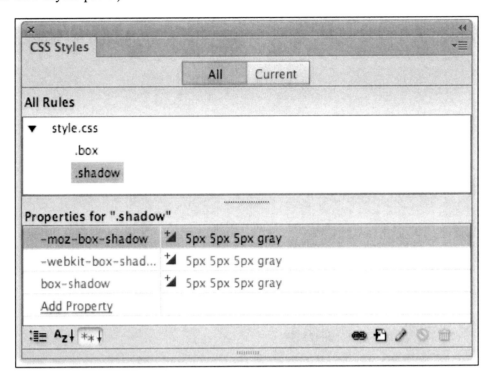

Text shadow

The text-shadow effect is very similar to the box-shadow effect, except that it is applied to text and not boxes. And, for whatever reason, unlike the box-shadow effect that requires a special prefix, the text-shadow effect does not require vendor prefixes.

The parameters for the text-shadow effect are the same as those for the box-shadow effect, where you define four values: x-offset, y-offset, blur distance, and color. Without the hassle of creating three versions of the effect, the following CSS code can be used to define a text shadow with 5 pixels of horizontal and vertical offset, a blur value of 5, and a gray color:

```
.text_shadow {

  text-shadow: 5px 5px 5px gray;
}
```

The `text-shadow` effect settings in the preceding example produce an effect like the following:

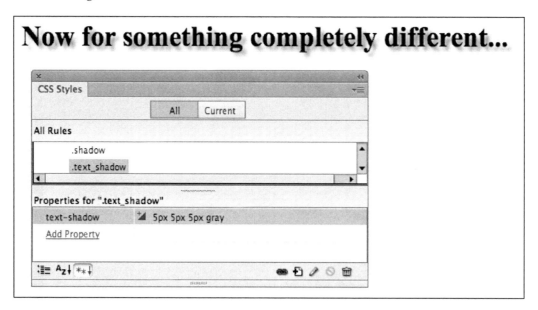

Creating a text outline

As alluded to earlier in this chapter, there is no such thing as a "text outline" effect. But there *is* a way to apply text outlines using the `text-shadow` effect. Generally, this involves matching the text color of the "outlined" type with the page background and then defining a particularly thin, black "shadow" with no blur at all that looks like an outline.

Creating effective outline effects requires stacking additional defining parameters in order to stack up very thin "shadows" both above and below and to the right and left of the text to which the style is applied. For example, when applied to text that sits on a white page background, the following class style combines (stacks) three different sets of parameters to create an outline effect.

```
.outline {
text-shadow: 0 1px 0 black, 0 -1px 0 black, 1px 0 0 black, -1px 0 0
black;
color: white;
}
```

Here's how that looks in a browser and in the **CSS Styles** panel.

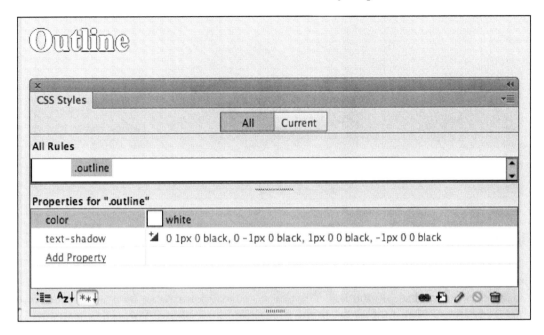

 Essentially, the preceding code generates a thin (1 pixel) "shadow" below the text, a second "shadow" below the text, and a third (1 pixel) thick "shadow" above the text. For a thicker outline, you could increase the pixel values uniformly to 2 pixels.

CSS3 transforms

The four CSS3 transitions `scale` (resize), `translate` (move), `rotate`, and `skew` are applied to selected content as *effects*. That is to say, they change the display or appearance of objects but not their underlying properties.

These transformations make it possible to present distortions of text or images that, before the advent of CSS3, was normally done through images—by using an image of text to present that text skewed, rotated, or scaled.

Rather than pushing my written communication skills beyond their limits, let's take advantage of the following figure to illustrate these four transitions:

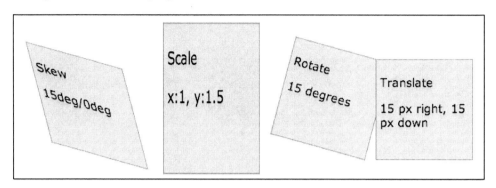

When to use transforms

The skew and rotate transforms can be used to present text or images in an intriguing and unique way, while maintaining the user's ability to select (and copy, paste, click on, and so on) the *text*. The translate transform can be used to place one block of content over another (as in the preceding illustration). The scale transform can be used to stretch or resize type or images.

When images overlap

When two <div> tags overlap, the one that appears in front will be the one with the highest z-index value. You can set the z-index in the **CSS Styles** panel.

In many instances, these effects work well as interactive animation, where a visitor triggers the transform by hovering over an object with his or her mouse. We'll explore that technique as the final element of this chapter.

As with the CSS3 effects explored earlier in this chapter, transitions can be applied to a wide range of tags such as heading tags (<h1>, <h2>, and so on) and images (using the <img> tag). Or more typically, class styles are defined to apply these transitions.

How to generate transition coding in Dreamweaver CS6

Before examining the relatively basic syntax necessary for defining a transform, let's revisit the controversy I tried to stir up earlier in this chapter over two possible approaches for squeezing the most out of Dreamweaver CS6's limited but helpful tools for generating CSS3 code.

To review and expand on the choices: you *cannot* define transforms in the **CSS Rule Definition** dialog, but you can apply CSS2 (earlier) styles in this way—rules such as background color, font definition, and so on. But, we would search in vain through the categories in Dreamweaver's **CSS Rule Definition** dialog for skew, scale, transform, or rotate. So the following two choices remain:

- Type the CSS code in the **Split** or **Code** view directly into the CSS file
- Use the limited resources of the **CSS Styles** panel to define the transforms

I'll let you jump back and review the more detailed discussion earlier in the chapter for a step-by-step walkthrough of how to either enter code in the CSS file you are working with or define styles using the **CSS Styles** panel. But there is one new factor to examine here: you get a bit more help in the **CSS Styles** panel defining transform parameters than you do for the effects (such as shadows) explored earlier in this chapter.

Here's how that additional help works: in the course of adding a rule to a style in the **CSS Styles** panel, if you enter one of the transform options (-webkit-transform, -moz-transform, or -o transform) at the bottom of the **CSS Styles** panel, Dreamweaver supplies a popup in the second column in the panel with various transform options, as shown in the following screenshot:

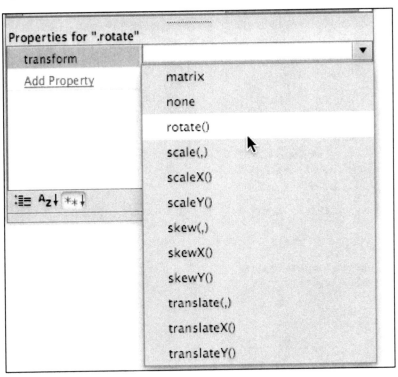

The bottom line is that you have to decide which environment is more comfortable for you to generate the CSS3 code for transforms. While exploring the specific transforms in the remainder of this chapter, I'll give away my own choice (just typing code in the **Code** view). But particularly when you are becoming familiar with the CSS3 code for transforms, you might find the popup help in the **CSS Styles** panel helpful.

Resizing with scale

Scaling is defined by two parameters, namely x and y. The x value defines how much width to increase (or with a negative value decrease), and the y value applies to the height. Values are normally multipliers, so that a value of 2 = 200%, means doubling the size, and a value of .5 = 50%, means reducing the size to half of the original value.

The following lines of code apply a `scale` transform that leaves the width of the object unchanged but increases the height by 50 percent:

```
-webkit-transform: scale(1,1.5);

-moz-transform: scale(1,1.5);

-o-transform: scale(1,1.5);
transform: scale(1,1.5);
```

Here's a sample of a class style (called `.scale`) that incorporates the preceding code and defines a class style that generates a 125-pixel square box (before rescaling) that can be scaled:

```
.scale {

  height: 125px;

  width: 125px;

  background-color: yellow;


  -webkit-transform: scale(1,1.5);

  -moz-transform: scale(1,1.5);

  -o-transform: scale(1,1.5);
   transform: scale(1,1.5);

  float: left;
```

```
   margin: 15px;

   padding:5px;

   border:1px solid #F00

}
```

Floating the box

In this example, the `float` attribute allows us to arrange a bunch of these, or similar, boxes in a single row.

Moving with translate

The `translate` transform moves objects from where they are placed on the page. As noted earlier, this can be an effective technique for having boxes, including boxes of selectable text, overlap on a page.

The syntax for the `translate` transform is similar to that for the `scale` transform except that the first parameter, that is, the x value defines how far to the right (left, if you use a negative value) and the y value defines how far down (up if you use a negative value) the object will move. Values are normally defined in pixels.

Here's the same class style we used as an example for the `scale` transform in the previous section, but with the `translate` transform set to move the object 35 pixels to the left and 15 pixels down:

```
.translate {

  height: 125px;

  width: 125px;

  background-color: yellow;

  transform: translate(-35px,15px);

  -webkit-transform: translate(-35px,15px);

  -moz-transform: translate(-35px,15px);

  -o-transform: translate(-35px,15px);
```

```
    float: left;

    margin: 15px;

    padding:5px;

    border:1px solid #F00


}
```

Applying rotation

The `rotate` transform is perhaps the simplest to define – there is only one parameter called the rotation angle. This angle can be positive (rotates clockwise) or negative (rotates counterclockwise).

An example of code that rotates an object 15 degrees clockwise is as follows:

```
transform: rotate(15deg);

-webkit-transform:rotate(15deg);

-moz-transform:rotate(15deg);


-o-transform:rotate(15deg);
```

An example of a class style that rotates an object 15 degrees with the same size and other attributes of the examples we've used previously is as follows:

```
.rotate {

  height: 125px;

  width: 125px;

  background-color: yellow;

  transform: rotate(15deg);

  -webkit-transform:rotate(15deg);

  -moz-transform:rotate(15deg);

  -o-transform:rotate(15deg);
```

```
    float: left;

    margin: 15px;

    padding:5px;

    border:1px solid #F00


}
```

Caution – leave space for rotate (and skew)

When you rotate an object (or, as we will see, if you skew
it), the object will overlap with nearby objects. Typically
(unless such an overlap is part of the design), this is
addressed by adding margin values to the object style
large enough to prevent an overlap.

Creating a skew transition

The skew transform is perhaps defined by two parameters separated by a comma.
The first defines the x-axis (horizontal) transform in degrees, and the second value
defines vertical distortion. If you use zero as a value for one of the two axes, the
result is a parallelogram as shown in the following screenshot:

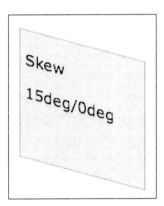

Here's an example of code for a class tag that applies the yellow background, red
border, and other attributes of our previous examples that skews an object 15
degrees on the box's axes:

```
    transform: rotate(15deg);

    -webkit-transform:rotate(15deg);
```

```
-moz-transform:rotate(15deg);

-o-transform:rotate(15deg);
```

And the following is an example of a class style that rotates an object 15 degrees, with the same size and other attributes of the examples we've used previously:

```
.skew {

  height: 125px;

  width: 125px;

    background-color: yellow;

  transform: skew(15deg,15deg);

  -webkit-transform: skew(15deg,15deg);

  -moz-transform: skew(15deg,15deg);

  -o-transform: skew(15deg,15deg);

  float: left;

  margin: 25px;

  padding:5px;

  border:1px solid #F00;}
```

Other CSS3 transform effects

In addition to the two-dimensional (2D) transform effects of CSS3 that we have explored in this chapter, there are other three-dimensional transforms in emerging states of support. They are, in general, not supported by any browsers except the WebKit set (SafariLimit), and from what I've been able to understand, at this point they are not that applicable without additional JavaScript that animates them.

That said, stay tuned. The world of CSS3 transforms is one of constant motion and development, and 3D transforms may gain broader support and become more accessible to developers.

Compound transforms

You can combine as many as all four transforms into a single transform rule. For example, to create a transform that applies `skew` (5 degrees on both the x and y axes), `scale` (multiples of 1.5 on both the x and y axes), and `rotate` (45 degrees), with a prefix that works with WebKit browsers, you would use the following code:

```
-webkit-transform: skew(5deg,5deg) scale(1.5, 1.5) rotate(45deg);
```

As transforms tend to apply rather radical changes to objects, and given that `skew` and `rotate` create similar effects, the aesthetics and accessibility that warrant combining multiple transforms in a single object are limited, but available.

Interactive effects and transforms

Having surveyed and walked through the process of creating and applying CSS3 effects and transforms, we turn now to one of the most exciting, dynamic aspects of these new style features: **interactivity**.

By interactivity, we mean that an object or elements of a page react to a visitor's action with their own action. A visitor hovers over an object, and that object moves, resizes, rotates, skews, develops a shadow, becomes semitransparent, or undergoes some other change.

There are two basic techniques for combining interactivity with effects and transforms. One is to use JavaScript and write or generate code that combines with transforms and effects. Combining JavaScript with effects and transforms can be a very powerful technique for creating interactivity on the level that can be generated, for example, using Flash.

The other, more accessible technique is to avail ourselves of the widely supported and easy-to-use `:hover` pseudo-class. If you're familiar with defining a "hover" state for a link, where a link takes on a unique appearance when hovered over, you have a basic idea of how this is going to work. And, we'll walk through that in more detail in the following sections.

Limitations of using effects with JavaScript

There are several definite limitations to creating interactive effects and transforms with JavaScript that places it beyond the scope of what we can address in this book. The first is that, in order to implement this approach, one needs to know JavaScript, and while that knowledge is available in thick books, through massive online resources, and with pay-to-use tools that generate JavaScript, it is well beyond what I could cover in this chapter, let alone this book. Further, JavaScript is not universally supported in browsing environments, and much of the appeal of HTML5 and CSS3 is that with proper accounting for non-HTML5 environments, nearly everything we are exploring in this book will work or at least not cause harm in any browsing environment.

Dreamweaver's underrated but also under-supported tool for generating JavaScript, the Behaviors panel, does not support CSS3 effects and transforms and so is, as yet, impotent when it comes to combining JavaScript effects and transforms.

We've partly enumerated the drawbacks (and plusses) for combining JavaScript with CSS3 effects and transforms because you're likely to encounter examples, models, and much discussion on the web among developers exploring the cutting edge of CSS3 and combining their work with JavaScript.

Interactivity with the :hover pseudo-class

There is, however, a much more accessible tool for applying interactive effects and transforms: the :hover pseudo-class.

Pseudo-classes are CSS modifiers that define the appearance of a web page object depending on the state of an object. They are best known for, and most widely applied as, modifiers on links.

For example, unvisited links on a web page are displayed as underlined in blue by default, visited links as underlined in purple, and active links as underlined in red. These parameters are easily changed in Dreamweaver's **CSS Styles** panel. And, they are supported in every modern browser and even in older ones.

But in addition to the :visited and :link :active pseudo-class styles (pseudo-classes), there is another, more dynamic state called :hover. This definable state applies to anything on a page that a visitor hovers his or her mouse over.

By applying effects and transforms to the hover state of an object, you can make it interact in a defined way with a visitor's mouse actions.

Animating CSS3 transforms in Dreamweaver

Let's now walk through exactly how CSS transforms and effects work with the
:hover pseudo-class.

The basic concept is that you define a :hover pseudo-class for the object you wish to
transform when being hovered over. This object can be an HTML tag (like <img>) or
a <div> tag (either class or ID).

In the case of the <img> tag, for instance, this line of code in the CSS file would define
a scale transform, increasing the height and width by 10 percent when the image is
hovered over:

```
img:hover   {

  -webkit-transform: scale(1.1,1.1);
}
```

Or taking another example — a div tag — the following code would cause a class style
container named .box to rotate 45 degrees when hovered over:

```
.box:hover {

  -webkit-transform:rotate(45deg)
}
```

Producing an effect like the following:

Example – create an animated effect and transform

This recipe creates a class style box that can be reused repeatedly on a page that displays a CSS3 effect and a CSS3 transform when hovered over. As such, it is an easily adaptable recipe—you can use the information in this chapter to substitute different effects and transforms that we'll use in the recipe.

In our particular scenario, we'll apply rounded corners and enlarge the box slightly when it is hovered over.

Putting the pieces in place

Here's what you need to have in place before diving into this recipe: you need to have a Dreamweaver site defined. Jump back to *Chapter 1*, *Creating Sites and Pages with Dreamweaver CS6*, and review the discussion and steps there for creating a Dreamweaver site.

With your site defined, you're ready! Everything we need is right here in Dreamweaver CS6. Let's first set up the files we need:

1. Navigate to **File | New** to open the **New Document** dialog. Choose **Blank Page** in the **Category** column, **HTML** in the **Page Type** column, and **<none>** in the **Layout** column. From the **DocType** popup, choose **HTML5**. The **Attach CSS File** box should be blank at this point. With the new file defined, click on **Create** to create a new, blank Dreamweaver page.

2. Enter Hover in the title area of the **Document** toolbar. Navigate to **File | Save** and assign a filename. Let's use the hover.html file.

3. Next, we'll create the CSS file that will hold our styles—particularly the CSS3 effect and transform styles that we'll be using. Navigate to **File | New**. The **New Document** dialog opens.

4. Select **CSS** in the **Page Type** category and click on the **Create** button. Save the CSS file; use the filename hover.css. A blank CSS page opens.

5. Select the HTML file. You can do this from the files tabs at the top of the Dreamweaver **Document** window. Or to avoid any possible confusion (given we have two similarly named files open), click on the **Window** menu and click on the `hover.html` file.

6. In the HTML page (you can be in any of the three views, but the **Design** view works fine), navigate to **Window** | **CSS Styles** to display the **CSS Styles** panel (if that panel is not visible).

7. Click on the **Attach Style Sheet** link icon at the bottom of the **CSS Styles** panel, and navigate to and link the `hover.css` stylesheet file. The (empty) stylesheet file appears in the **CSS Styles** panel. You can see all the elements we've defined so far, and your screen should, at this point, look like the one shown in the following screenshot:

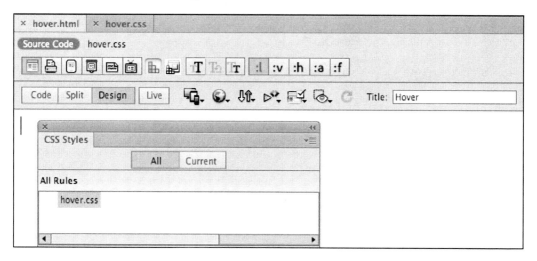

8. Click on the **New CSS Rule** icon at the bottom of the **CSS Styles** panel to open the **New CSS Rule** dialog. From the **Selector Type** popup choose **Class**, and in the **Selector Name** box type `box`. In the **Rule Definition** area if `hover.css` is not already selected, choose it from the **Rule Definition** popup. Click on **OK** to open the **CSS Rule Definition for .box in hover.css** dialog.

9. In the **Background** category of the **CSS Rule Definition** dialog, choose a light colored background color (such as yellow). In the **Box** category, apply the following rules as illustrated in the following screenshot. Don't click on **OK** yet! We'll define a border next.

- ° **Width**: **200 px**
- ° **Height**: **200 px**
- ° **Float**: **left**
- ° **Padding**: **25** (for all)
- ° **Margin**: **50** (for all)

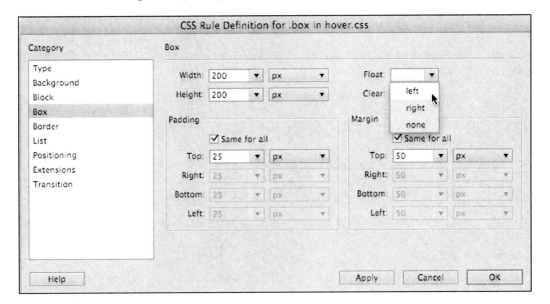

A note on the settings

We're creating a 200-pixel square box, which is a nice size for holding a sidebar message or picture and caption. We floated it to the left-hand side so other content can be wrapped around the box on the right-hand side. The large margin and padding provides plenty of flexibility for effects that might expand the box or impinge on the space of nearby elements.

10. Next, let's create a kind of fun border. In the **Border** category of the **CSS Rule Definition** dialog, define the border as dashed, thick, and red, as shown in the following screenshot. Then click on **OK** to create the style rule.

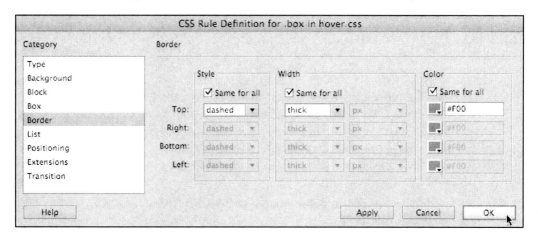

11. Let's place one (or -- your option -- more than one) instance of this class style on the page now. Navigate to **Insert | Layout Objects** to open the **Insert Div Tag** dialog. Choose **box** from the **Class** popup and click on **OK**. Note that you can do this repeatedly if you wish to use this box as a page design element, as shown in the following screenshot. You can also use this figure to double-check the rules for the .box class style in the **CSS Styles** panel.

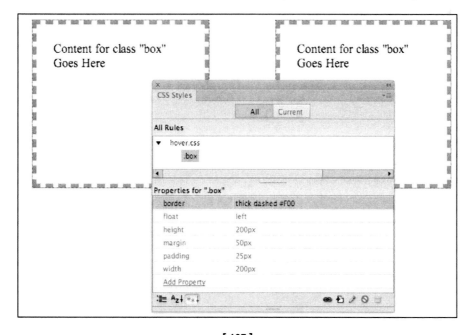

Using a hover class style to animate effects

We can now define the :hover pseudo-class style to animate this box with scaling and rounded corners. We were able to create a sized, floated box with a defined border using Dreamweaver CS6's **CSS Styles** panel and dialogs. For the CSS3 styles required in the following steps, we won't be quite so lucky. We will define a style using the **CSS Styles** panel, but we will have to enter the CSS3 style code ourselves using just Dreamweaver CS6's code hints.

1. Click on the **New CSS Rule** icon at the bottom of the **CSS Styles** panel to open the **New CSS Rule** dialog. From the **Selector Type** popup choose **class**, and in the **Selector Name** box type .box:hover. In the **Rule Definition** area, if hover.css is not already selected, choose it from the **Rule Definition** popup. Click on **OK** to open the **CSS Rule Definition dialog for .box:hover in hover.css** dialog.

2. As the rules we need are not available in the **CSS Rule Definition** dialog, click on **OK** to save the style .box:hover without any rules at the current stage.

3. Navigate to **Window | hover.css** to open the CSS styles file in Dreamweaver's **Code** view. Refer to the following code to define a scale transition that bumps the size of the box up to a noticeable, but not obnoxious, 2 percent and applies subtle rounded corners to the box. The code makes this effect accessible for Safari (-webkit), IE9 (generic), Opera (-o), and Firefox (-moz) users.

The code specifically for the .box:hover style is as follows:

```css
.box:hover {

  -webkit-transform:scale(1.02);

  -webkit-border-radius: 10px;

  -transform:scale(1.02);

  -border-radius: 10px;

  -o-transform:scale(1.02);

  -o-border-radius: 10px;

  -moz-transform:scale(1.02);

  -moz-border-radius: 10px;

}
```

4. Save the CSS file (navigate to **File | Save**). Use the **Window** menu to return to the **hover.html** page. Test the effect and transform in the **Live** view, along with other browsers using the **Preview** option of the **File** menu in the browser. The following screenshot shows the effect in Firefox — the middle box displays as slightly larger with rounded corners.

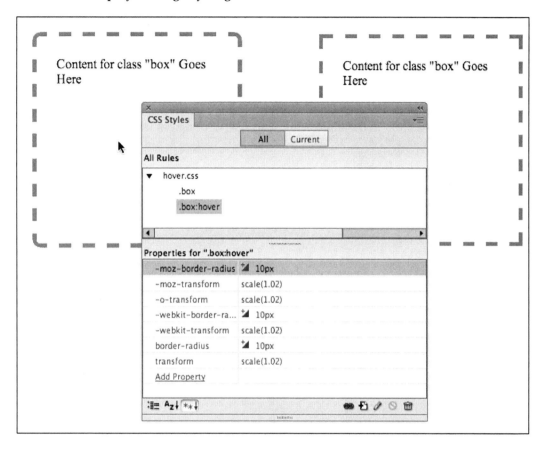

Once again, this is a highly adaptable recipe and can be the basis for creating page layout elements that interact with visitors hovering over them. You could, for example, replace scale with rotate, skew, or even translate to alter the transform. And you could replace the border-radius effect with shadows or opacity changes.

Summary

In this chapter, we covered a wide range of effects and transforms available with the emergence of the CSS3 standards for stylesheets. Those "standards" are inconsistent, so there is a need to provide alternate (prefixed) rules for different browsers.

These transforms and effects are useful as design tools in their own right, and they are even more dynamic design factors when made interactive by defining `:hover` pseudo-class elements that cause them to appear when (and only when) an object is hovered over.

Dreamweaver CS6 provides a basic framework for defining and applying CSS3 transforms and effects. We examined Dreamweaver's limited CSS3 tools, like the ability to use code hints in the **Code** view and useful prompts for transforms in the **CSS Styles** panel.

In the next chapter of this book, we explore adding "native" audio and video to web pages using HTML5. Native audio and video runs directly in a browser without plugin players (such as Windows Media Player, QuickTime Player, or Flash Player).

5
Embedding HTML5 Native Audio and Video

In this chapter, we walk through how to add audio and video to web pages using HTML5. The advantage of embedding media using HTML5 in Dreamweaver is that it does not require any external player to work. For browsers that support the HTML5 Audio or Video element, native media is the most elegant way to present audio and video online.

Dreamweaver makes adding HTML5 audio relatively painless—without extensive knowledge of or worrying about HTML coding.

Native media and compatibility

Before launching our journey to embedding media with HTML5, let's step back for just a moment to survey the terrain. Until HTML5, if you wanted to listen to audio or watch video from a website, you had to do so through the agency of a browser plugin of one kind or another. That plugin might have been QuickTime Player (typically on a Mac), Windows Media Player (typically on a Windows computer), Flash, a plugin supplied by your hardware manufacturer, or some other program.

Since users listened to audio with the aid of plugins (such as Windows Media Player or QuickTime Player), web designers had almost no control over what appeared onscreen when a user listened to an audio. HTML5 provides what is called **native** audio (as well as native video). Native video does not require a plugin. The player and controls still vary some depending on the browsing environment, but with HTML5, the audio player is *relatively* standardized.

There are two compatibility issues in presenting HTML5 audio and video: 1) a visitor's browser must be HTML5 compliant; and 2) a visitor's browser must support the particular audio format to which the audio or video is saved. So, in walking through the process of presenting HTML5 audio, we'll explore how to handle both of these compatibility issues.

I'll return to compatibility issues in more detail separately for audio and video as we walk through the process of embedding native audio, and then native video, using Dreamweaver.

Laying the groundwork

Support for HTML5 audio and video in Dreamweaver CS6 is still a bit primitive. If you update Dreamweaver with Creative Cloud, more HTML5 elements (including audio and video) are available from the **Insert** menu (or **Insert** toolbar). But all versions of Dreamweaver CS6 (and 5.5) provide valuable code-hinting in **Code** (or **Split**) view, and that's the approach we will take here since it works in any Dreamweaver CS6 environment. And, besides, it is good to be exposed to and understand the audio and video tag syntax.

Let's quickly review two essential things you need to work with HTML5 media in Dreamweaver:

* If you haven't already, make sure you have a Dreamweaver site defined. This is an essential first step. To learn how to define a site, you can take a look at *Chapter 1, Creating Sites and Pages with Dreamweaver CS6,* of this book to find out how to do so.
* Collect media files. For audio: MP3, OGG, and WebM format audio files. For video: h.264 (often with an .mp4 filename extension), OGG, or WebM. You are going to want to have all three versions of your video files—h.264, OGG, and WebM. You can use the free program **Switch** (http://www.nch.com.au/switch/index.html) to translate files from one audio format to another. For video conversion, you can use the free program **Online-Convert**, available for download at http://video.online-convert.com/.

With this as an introduction, let's turn to the specific processes of embedding native HTML5 audio and video, in Dreamweaver.

Preparing native audio

The first thing we need to do, before we can put them on our website, is make our audio files HTML5-ready.

Before shifting through various audio formats to figure out which one goes with which browser, let me provide a very basic overview of audio compression.

Audio compression

You probably are familiar with at least some of the popular audio formats such as MP3, WAV, AIFF, and so on. Raw, uncompressed audio files, in the WAV (for Windows) and AIFF (for Macs) formats, provide the highest available online audio sound quality. But these files are very large, and download too slowly for most users. MP3 audio files, on the other hand, are substantially smaller in file size.

A compression algorithm is used to squeeze extra data out of files as they are converted to MP3. And for most listeners, and most audio files, MP3 quality is sufficient. Thus, when we talk about making audio files available online, we are often talking about compressed audio files in formats such as MP3. Another compressed file format is the OGG format.

Browser support for audio files

MP3 and OGG are the two most widely used formats for compressed audio. Since uncompressed audio takes much longer to download, compressed audio (MP3 and OGG) are preferable for almost all downloadable audio.

Which compressed audio format works in all browsers? Unfortunately, neither one works in all browsers. The five most popular browsers—Internet Explorer, Firefox, Chrome, Safari, and Opera—support HTML5 Audio, but different browsers support different formats.

Which audio formats are supported by which browsers changes over time, but at the time of writing this chapter, the breakdown was:

* Internet Explorer 9 and newer: MP3
* Firefox 4.0 and newer: OGG
* Google Chrome 6 and newer: Both
* Apple Safari 5 and newer: MP3
* Opera 10.6 and newer: OGG

W3Schools.com keeps an updated list of browser support for audio formats at http://www.w3schools.com/html/html5_audio.asp. But as exactly as I can predict the future, you're going to have to provide both MP3 and OGG audio if you want to reach the overwhelming majority of users.

The most reliable and "standards-compliant" solution for presenting HTML5 audio is to provide the option of both the HTML5 compressed audio formats, MP3 and OGG. That is the solution we'll explore next.

Embedding an HTML5 audio element in a Dreamweaver web page

Once we've laid the groundwork, we are ready to get started. Use the following steps to embed an Audio element into an open Dreamweaver HTML5 page:

1. In the **Code** part of the **Split** view, place your cursor right after the **<body>** tag and hit *Enter* (or *Return* on a Mac) to create a new line of code.

2. Start typing <au and press *Tab* and the HTML5 pack will auto-complete that into the beginning of the <audio> tag, as shown in the following screenshot:

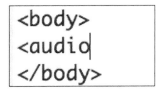

3. Place your cursor right after the word audio and press the *Space bar*. A pop-up menu will appear again. Type the letter s and then double-click src in the list. This is code for the source, as in, where the file will come from.

4. When you select src, a **Browse** link will appear. Double-click on the **Browse** link to open the **Select File** dialog, as shown in the following screenshot:

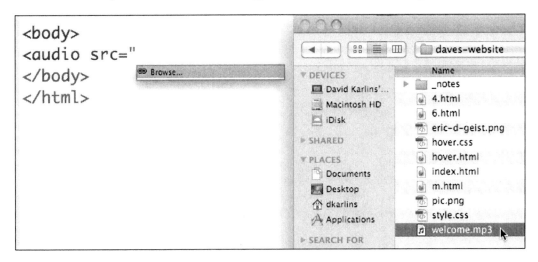

5. Find the audio file you copied before, in our case an MP3 file (but it could be WAV or OGG). Select that file by double-clicking on it.

6. You want to have a controller, or player, for this audio, so we'll set a parameter to display one. Press the *Space bar* again, and this time type c, which in this case will be for controls. Double-click on **controls**, and then when a pop-up box appears, double-click **controls** again, as shown in the following screenshot:

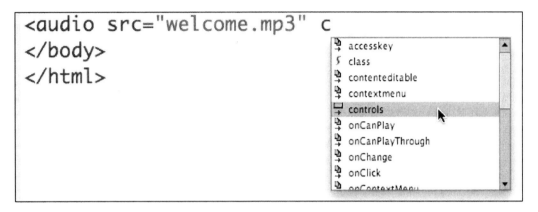

7. Close the opening audio tag by typing >.

8. Finally, type </ to allow Dreamweaver to auto-complete to </audio>, which will complete the audio element with a closing tag.

Now we want to preview the file, which we can only do in Safari or Opera, assuming you chose an MP3. To preview in Safari, navigate to **File | Preview in Browser | Safari**. It should look like the following screenshot:

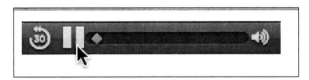

If we had used an OGG file, we could do the same steps, but we would now have to preview in Firefox instead.

Alternative audio options

So now you have audio on your page. But two things are missing:

- First, your audio player doesn't have many special features.

- Second, not everyone who visits the sites will be able to access the audio file. You should provide different HTML5-supported audio formats as options for different browsing environments since, as we've identified earlier, not all HTML5-friendly browsers support the same audio file formats.

Let's start with the challenge of providing alternate audio file formats. As we've noted, some HTML5-compliant browsing environments support the MP3 file format, others support the OGG format, and remaining support WebM.

So, we can make our audio more accessible by providing a second source file. That way, an HTML5-compliant browser can find and play the file format that meshes with that browser.

To do this, we'll vary the HTML we created earlier to separate the player control code from the audio source code. The code looks similar to the following block of code:

```
<audio controls="controls">
    <source src="audio.ogg" type="audio/ogg" />
    <source src="audio.mp3" type="audio/mpeg" />
</audio>
```

In the preceding code, you replace audio.ogg or audio.mp3 with your own audio filenames.

For those users whose browsers don't interpret HTML5, such as users of older versions of Internet Explorer or users on older browsers, we will want to provide an alternative method of accessing the audio. To do this, we can create a link to our audio file. If we do this, when the link is clicked the audio file will open in its own browser user. The browser will then use a plugin player such as QuickTime, Flash, or Windows Media to play the audio file. It is not the most elegant solution, but it will work.

To do this, we can add a line of code to the HTML we just explored. This line of code creates text that will appear in browsers that do not interpret (support) the HTML5 <audio> tag, and can link to a page that presents audio in a legacy format such as QuickTime, Windows Media, or FLV.

The code looks similar to the following:

```
<audio controls="controls">

  <source src="sound.ogg" type="audio/ogg" />

  <source src="sound.mp3" type="audio/mpeg" />
Your browser does not support the HTML5 audio element but you can hear
the audio file <a href="sound.html">here</a>.
</audio>
```

This last line of code, which begins with `Your browser...`, links to an HTML page (`sound.html`) that can be used to present the legacy audio format that will play in a plugin software on older browsers.

Adding play parameters

Now that (almost) everyone can access our audio, let's look at what other parameters we can use to add features to our `audio` element.

When we added the code `controls="controls"` in defining our source file, we added a control parameter. If you played with the controller in Safari when you tested it out, you have already discovered that this controller will let us play, pause, mute, and restart our MP3. We can also use the bar, or scrubber, to move around in the audio track, rewind, or fast-forward.

There are four significant HTML5 Audio parameters we might want to use. To enable each of these parameters, we will want to use the HTML5 code hints the same way we did to enable controls:

- `controls`: This property displays controls to start, pause, stop, or change volume in the audio player.

- `loop`: This plays the audio file repeatedly, or in a loop. To enable this looping, place your cursor after the code `controls="controls"` and press the *Space bar* to activate the code hints. Type 1 and then double-click on `loop` to add the `loop` code .

- `autoplay`: This starts the audio file immediately when someone opens the page, as opposed to the viewer having to press **Play**, the way we did with the controller. You can have both `loop` and `autoplay` enabled at the same time. To make the audio play automatically, place your cursor after the code `controls="controls"` and press the *Space bar* to activate the code hints. Double-click on `autoplay` to add the code `autoplay =""`. For autoplaying an audio file, you don't need to put anything between the quotation marks in the code, the way we did with `controls` and `loop`. Just adding the code enables it, as shown in the following screenshot:

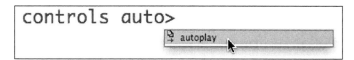

 Mobile devices (including iOS Apple devices) and some versions of Android mobile operating system do not support `autoplay`, which argues for including `controls`.

- **preload**: This property starts downloading the audio file when the page is open, before **Play** is clicked. This is not relevant if we're using `autoplay`, since it will load immediately either way, but when we are not using `autoplay`, it allows the audio file to launch quicker when a visitor clicks **Play**. I recommend not using this option since it delays the opening of a page in many mobile environments. If you want to preload the track, once again you just place your cursor after the code `controls="controls"` and press the *Space bar* to activate the code hints. Type p and then double-click `preload`, and then double-click on `auto` to add the code `preload="auto"`.

- There are two other possible variables for the `preload` property: `none` and `metadata`. The `none` variable specifies explicitly not to preload the file, while `metadata` specifies to just preload the metadata information (for example, information about song title, author, and so on of an audio file).

You can enable multiple parameters at the same time. Just press *Space bar* after the code `controls="controls"` each time to activate HTML5 code hints, and then repeat for whatever other code you want. So you can have a track that autoplays and loops too, for example.

Remember what will make the most sense for the audio you have and the preferences of visitors to your site. Keep in mind that many visitors will not appreciate sound automatically playing when they enter the main page of your site. They may be at work, or may just not want the sound on. Unless it is a linked page they expect sound on, it is more considerate to your visitors to have audio be something they can choose to turn on, rather than something they must choose to turn off.

Embedding HTML5 audio

In the following section, we'll walk through, step-by-step, how to embed an MP3 audio file using the HTML5 Audio element, and provide an option for visitors whose browsers do not support HTML5. I'll assume you are working in a Dreamweaver site and that you have a file open, saved as an HTML5 web page (saving the file first is important to ensure the integrity of the link to the audio file). And, that you have an MP3 audio file ready to embed.

With those pieces in place, these steps will work:

1. In the Dreamweaver Document window, jump into **Split** view, and in the **Code** side of the **Split** view, click where you wish to create a new line of code. This can be anywhere in between the `<body>` and `</body>` tags.

2. Start typing `<audio>`. A couple of letters into the process, you can press the *Tab* key to complete the beginning of the element. Then press your *Space bar*.

3. Double-click on **src** from the pop-up list, as shown here. A **Browse** link appears:

4. Double-click on the **Browse** link to open the **Select File** dialog and navigate to and choose the MP3 audio file.

5. Press the *Space bar* again, and double-click on **controls** in the code hints that appear. Double-click on **controls** again in the next code hint.

6. Type `</` and Dreamweaver will complete the closing element `</audio>`.

7. Now, to support non-HTML browsers, add a line of text on your web page with a link to the audio file you just embedded with the HTML5 `<audio>` tag. To do that, locate an insertion point (click with your mouse in the code side of **Split** view, just before the `</audio>` code that closes the Audio element. Type a closing angle bracket (>) to complete the element. Then type `Listen to the audio file` as regular HTML text, and use the **Properties** inspector to attach a link to the audio file for the text you embedded with the HTML5 `<audio>` tag.

 This code provides seamless HTML5 audio for HTML5-enabled browsers that can handle MP3 files, and a link to the MP3 file for everyone else.

Embedding native video

Next, we will learn how to add different kinds of video to web pages using HTML5 and Dreamweaver.

Online video is undergoing a radical evolution. Those changes can be very briefly summed up as the following: you don't need a plugin player anymore. Dreamweaver provides limited but valuable support for embedding this native video (so-called because it plays in the native browser environment without plugins).

We will learn how to use the HTML5 video element through several steps:

• Understanding the concept of native video, and how it relates to early evolutionary steps in the development of web video and also, which video formats work in which browsers.

• Creating HTML5-ready digital video files.

- Using the `<video>` tag to embed video with Dreamweaver.
- Providing alternative options for non-HTML5 compatible browsers.
- Defining additional video display parameters.

 We need to do each of these steps to make sure that the HTML5 video we include in our site will work in every browsing environment.

HTML5 video and Dreamweaver

To understand the challenges of presenting online video today, it is illuminating to frame things in the evolution of web video to this point. For one thing, older web videos are still an issue, as are older browsers. We have to address the challenge of presenting video in both new browsers that support current standards, and older browsers that do not.

Moreover, the current rather crazy state of competing online video formats won't make much sense without being anchored in an understanding of how this current state of things emerged.

To sort all this out, it is useful to divide emergent online video into three phases.

Early video formats

The first stage of online video was characterized by a diffusion of different, non-compatible video formats and players. Apple's QuickTime video played in QuickTime player, which came with Apple's Safari browser. Microsoft's Internet Explorer played various Microsoft video formats such as AVI or WMF. Typically, web designers included QuickTime video in a site with the expectation that only users on Macs would be able to see the video, or included Windows Media Formats such as WMV or AVI, with the expectation that only users with Windows Media Player (appropriately updated) could handle the video. During this phase, other formats, such as RealMedia's video and player gained traction for a time.

In this early phase, the lack of a single online video format was one marginalizing factor impacting web video. In addition, the absence of a critical mass of users with high-speed connections made online video less attractive. Low quality video and audio display in laptops and digital devices was another factor. Web video from being the integral component of websites that it is today and a corresponding lack of quality online video content made web video something of a marginal element in web design.

Culturally and technically, web video was, at this point, something of an "outsider" in web browsing experience—requiring long waits for downloads, and explanation to users on how to watch video, as illustrated in the following site that I created for the Himalayan Fair in 2002:

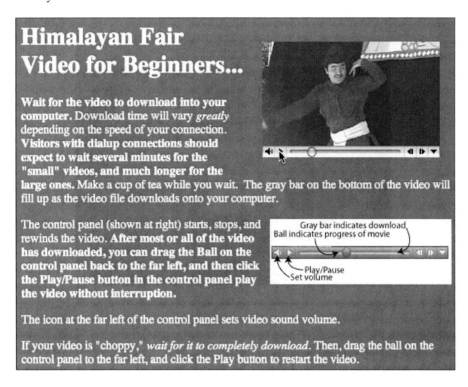

In terms of HTML and Dreamweaver technique, the `<embed>` tag was used to place video on a page. This tag allowed some designer control over player controls and other parameters (such as `autoplay`) but how (and if) the video played was mainly defined by a user's browser, and the plugins he/she had installed in that browser.

Flash video (FLV)

Phase two in the evolution of online video, as we're delineating things here, marked the integration of video into every realm of every kind of website.

One critical factor in the move of video into the mainstream on the web was the emergence of Adobe's **Flash Video** (**FLV**) format and the widespread acceptance of Flash Player. FLV presents video in a highly compressed form—radically reducing file size (often by half compared to QuickTime) while maintaining good video and audio quality.

FLV files required the Flash Player, but during this phase of the Web, installation of the Flash Player was almost universal. Dreamweaver, particularly in CS4 and CS5, included nice, customizable menu-driven Flash Player design tools. Dreamweaver designers could choose from a variety of Flash Player skins as they embedded Flash Video. The following screenshot shows a minimalist player skin:

Intersecting with the rise of FLV and near-universal support for the Flash Player was the availability of high speed Internet connections, and the proliferation of video content. The instant popularity of YouTube, which featured FLV videos, was an expression of and an engine of these phenomena. These developments, which are still a major element of web video, transformed web video from marginal to mainstream.

In terms of HTML and Dreamweaver, FLV would be embedded in pages using the `<object>` tag. But the appearance of the video player and the properties of parameters such as autoplay or looping are defined in the **Properties** panel in Dreamweaver's **Document** window for a selected FLV video.

The main disadvantage of using FLV video is that it is not supported on the iPhone, iPod Touch, or iPad (or iPods). I'll explain how that situation developed next, along with the implications for web designers using video.

Apple devices and web video

The parameters of online video—with Flash Video as the cohering element—seemed defined, relatively stable, and globally accepted. Until...Steve Jobs published "Thoughts on Flash" in April, 2010. The essence of that letter was stating and making permanent Apple's position that it would never support the Flash Player on its i-gadgets:

> *"The mobile era is about low power devices, touch interfaces, and open web standards – all areas where Flash falls short. The avalanche of media outlets offering their content for Apple's mobile devices demonstrates that Flash is no longer necessary to watch video or consume any kind of web content."*

This decision came at a time when, despite Jobs' pronouncement, the bulk of online video, at sites such as Hulu and YouTube, for example, was in Flash Video. And people who tried to watch video from these sites typically got messages like the one shown in the following screenshot:

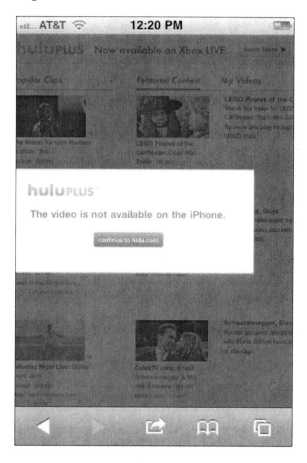

Apple threw its considerable weight behind the `h.264` format for packaging compressed video. This format essentially uses the same compression technology as Flash Video, but comes in a package that adapts player display and controls from a browser, not from a plugin player.

Setting aside the power politics and economics dimensions of this decision, the essential technical and design issues were that Apple did not want to expand limited energy resources in their digital devices on the Flash Player, and Apple argued that video players should be "native" to viewing environments, rather than global cross-platform interfaces like those in the Flash Player (that look essentially the same on every operating system and browser).

Within a year of Apple's announcement, the critical mass in providing online video had begun to tip towards native video. But FLV remains widely distributed online. Thus, web designers using Dreamweaver face the challenge of embedding native video.

Preparing native video files

Native video is presented in HTML5 with the `<video>` element (tag). Accomplishing that is our mission in this chapter, and shortly, we'll explore tools available in Dreamweaver for embedding video using that tag.

Before we do that, let's identify the two big challenges to developers in providing native video. One is that there is not one but three native video formats. The second challenge is that older versions of Internet Explorer (8 and earlier) do not support the HTML5 `<video>` element.

Native video formats

The three most widely supported native video formats are: MP4 (h.264), supported by Safari; Theora OGG, an open source video format supported by Mozilla Firefox; and WebM, supported by Google Chrome, Opera, and reportedly soon in Firefox.

The following is a more detailed breakdown of which browsers currently support which video formats:

- Ogg: Firefox, Chrome, Opera 10.5+
- h.264 (MP4): Internet Explorer 9+, Safari, older versions of Chrome, Apple's mobile devices, Android devices
- WebM: Chrome 6+, Opera 10.6+

But keep in mind, all this is a moving target.

As you can see, there is no video format supported by all major browsers. And in particular, Firefox and Chrome (with a combined substantial share of the browser market) do not support the h.264 video format.

We will solve this challenge by providing alternate videos, all with the same parameters (location, player control display, and so on).

Browsers that do NOT support HTML5

Providing alternate video formats will solve the problem of making our native video display in all HTML5 browsers. But older visions of Internet Explorer (pre-IE 9) do not support HTML5!

In the course of walking through the nits and grits of embedding native video, we'll build in backup support for browsers that do not support the HTML5 <video> tag. We'll do that by making a version of our video available in the FLV format.

Preparing HTML5 video for every scenario

If you choose to provide only one of the available popular video formats for the Web, you are going to exclude a large chunk of people from seeing your video. For example, if you elect to use the h.264 format supported on Apple mobile devices, that video cannot be viewed by the 30 percent or so of all users who are navigating the Web with Firefox. Conversely, if you provide Flash Video (FLV), your video can be watched in Firefox, but not by the highly-valued 5 percent of web browsers browsing on their i-devices.

Our challenge, then, is to supply fast-downloading, compressed web video that is supported in *every* browser (or at least every significant browsing environment).

No problem! By the end of this chapter, you'll be able to do just that in Dreamweaver.

Compressing video for the Web

Let's go back to our earlier discussion of the evolution of video for the Web. A key link in the chain was the development of powerful, effective compression for web video. It might be helpful to explain very briefly how this works.

Video animation—whether digital or old school analog (such as films)—is presented in frames. The more frames displayed per second, the smoother the animation.

Video compression reduces the size of a digital video not by reducing the number of frames, but by rationalizing the way frame data is saved. Say, for example, that you have a video of a person speaking against a background. It might well be the case that the background doesn't change throughout the video. Video compression software compacts the digital data necessary to present that video by organizing the data used to depict the background in such a way that it does not have to be repeated for each frame of the video.

 I'm using a very simple example here to help make a point, but the point is more broadly applicable, even to video with more complex backgrounds. And, as a general rule of thumb, compression reduces file size by about half, while maintaining the original quality.

In a typical workflow, you might start with video files in QuickTime's MOV format (or Microsoft's AVI format). These videos, straight from a video camera, or from video editing software, are not compressed. They could be presented directly online except that:

- They are unnecessarily large and double the download time
- Not all of them are supported by browsers unless those browsers have plugins added, and we're trying to get away from that

So, after you or someone else has created video in an uncompressed format, a key step in the process of preparing that video for the Web is to compress it.

Video compression – open source and proprietary

The four most popular compressed digital video formats used on the Web are roughly divided into two groups: open source, and proprietary. Proprietary formats are owned and licensed, while open source formats are free to the public.

WebM and Ogg Theora are free, open source video formats. To create them, you can use a variety of free encoding programs.

Flash Video (FLV) and h.264 are not open source but proprietary. To generate them, we can use Adobe Media Encoder.

While creating four additional (compressed) versions of an original uncompressed video (from a QuickTime or Windows Media format) is a bit of a hassle, it's doable.

Converting video to web formats with open source tools

There are a number of free downloadable applications that convert your (raw) QuickTime or Windows Media files to compressed Theora OGG or WebM.

 I'm currently using one called **Miro Video Converter** (www.mirovideoconverter.com), a nice, free downloadable application.

Whichever free video compression application you end up using, the process involves two steps: adding your video to the cache to be converted, and choosing an output format (such as h.264), as shown in the following screenshot (in this case with Miro Video Converter):

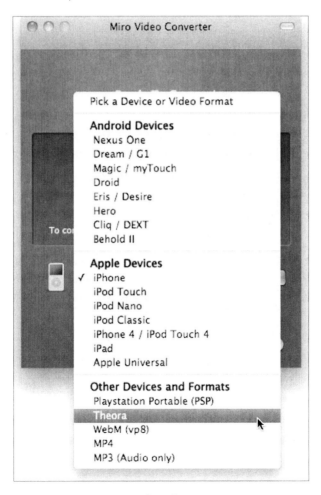

Of course, those two general steps will be performed differently depending on which open source video conversion program you end up using. In general, these free video compression applications are pretty no-frills. They don't provide options for editing, resizing, or tweaking the quality of compressed video. Thus, I advise using them to convert the open source versions of your web video (Theora OGG and WebM), but not the Flash Video (FLV) and h.264 (MP4) version of your video.

For that, I suggest taking advantage of Adobe Media Encoder that ships with nearly every version of Creative Suite.

Dreamweaver site management for HTML5 video

Now, having explored the process of preparing video for HTML5, let's briefly examine how to prepare to take maximum advantage of Dreamweaver in this process.

There are two ways Dreamweaver will assist in embedding HTML5 video. One way, which we'll get to shortly, is that Dreamweaver will provide helpful code hints that facilitate creating the HTML5 code we need.

But the other value of Dreamweaver in this process is that the site management tools will keep track of all the files we need, and most importantly, maintain the integrity of links we create between embedded video and the other files (CSS, possible JavaScript, embedded images, and so on) needed to make our page work properly in browsers.

So, as a critical next step, make sure you are working in a Dreamweaver website. As we've addressed this in previous chapters, we will review the bare-bones basics involved in doing that here in three easy steps:

1. If you are not working in a defined Dreamweaver site, navigate to **Site | New Site**. In the **Site Setup** dialog, give your new site a name and define a local site folder. Doing this defines a Dreamweaver site. Defining the Servers element of a site is not essential to embedding HTML5 video in Dreamweaver web pages, but defining the local site is.

2. Now create a new file, and save it within your defined site. To do that, navigate to **File | New** to open the **New Document** dialog. Select **Blank Page** in the **Category** column, **HTML** in the **Page Type** column, and **<none>** in the **Layout** column. Select **HTML5** from the **Doc Type** popup. Click on **Create** to create a new, blank Dreamweaver page.

3. For good housekeeping purposes to avoid the **Untitled** page title, enter a title in the **Title** area of the **Document** window (this can be any descriptive text).

4. Navigate to **File | Save** and assign a filename.

[By saving a file, we will be able to link a video using relative paths.]

Defining the HTML5 <video> element

Once you've prepared a Dreamweaver site, and created h.264, OGG, WebM, and FLV versions of your video, you have all the elements you need to embed native HTML5 video, and provide an alternative for browsers without support for HTML5.

In the following steps, you'll complete the process of placing video in an HTML5 web page.

We can't, regrettably, do this in **Design** view. Dreamweaver does not have **Design** view menu options for embedding HTML5 native video. But we can take advantage of two useful features in Dreamweaver's **Document** window: **Code hinting** and **Split view**. Code hinting will help us generate the HTML5 code we need, and Split view will allow us to preview at least some of the possible ways visitors will see our video as we create it.

Prerequisites

In order to review and re-emphasize the things, you need the following in place before creating HTML5 video in Dreamweaver:

- You should have prepared an h.264 (mp4); Theora (OGG); WebM (webm) and Flash Video (FLV) version of your video. You can elect to provide support for just one, or some of the first three HTML5-compatible formats. If you provide support for h.264 and OGG, you will have almost all modern browsers covered.

- You must create a Dreamweaver site and have an open page in the Dreamweaver **Document** window saved as an HTML5 file within your site. View the page in **Split** view.

- Copy all your video files into a folder within the site folder you defined. If you save your video files elsewhere, Dreamweaver will prompt you to make copies of the videos within your site folder, but it saves a step and simplifies things to create copies of the video files in the site folder at this stage.

Defining the <video> element

In your saved HTML5 page, place your cursor after the opening `<body>` tag. If you are embedding a video in a page with existing content, place your insertion point where the video should appear.

1. Type `<vi` and code hinting will then show the `<video>` tag.

2. Press *Tab* to complete the beginning of the `<video>` tag.

3. Use code hinting to add parameters for height, width, and controls. The height and width values can either match the original values of your video, or be larger or smaller. If the values are larger than the original video, the resolution of the video will be degraded. Including the `controls` parameter displays player controls (for play, pause, stop, and volume). The resulting code is as follows:

```
<video width="xxxpx" height="yyypx" controls>
```

(where xxx is the width of the video, and yyy is the height)

As we are going to support multiple video formats, we closed the `video` tag by typing here.

Defining video attributes

The HTML5 video controller normally displays a play button, a pause button, and a mute button, as well as a scrubber (a horizontal bar with a movable thumb to scroll backwards or forwards within video playback). Moreover, by default, HTML5 video controls display only when the user hovers his or her mouse pointer over the video, or when the video begins to play.

The most important video parameters are `height`, `width`, and `controls`. The `controls` parameter displays these player controls. The `height` and `width` values are followed by units of measurement, almost always pixels.

There are other useful HTML5 video parameters, which are as follows:

- `Audio=muted` turns off volume when the video begins to play
- `Autoplay=autoplay` launches the video automatically
- `Loop=loop` repeats the video
- `Preload=preload` loads the video when the page is opened, even before it is played
- `Poster=[filename]` (where `filename` is a PNG image file) displays artwork before the video is played

Settings for iOS: iPads cannot autoplay HTML5 videos, Apple doesn't allow it on its iOS devices, so don't rely on autoplay if your audience includes visitors on those devices. Also, preloading is appropriate for desktops and laptops, but too resource-intensive for mobile devices.

Even though preparing HTML5 video usually means presenting multiple video source files, the other attributes can be defined for all of them together. Moreover, normally, that is what you will want to do, since attributes such as video size, autoplay status, and so on will be the same regardless of what video file format a visitor views.

Each of these parameters is supported by code hinting, and we'll explore how that works in detail in the recipe at the end of this chapter.

Defining video source(s)

Each video source requires a separate line of HTML5 code. That code is generated in Dreamweaver (any version with the HTML5 Pack installed) with code hints.

To begin to define a video source, type `<sour`, as you do, code hinting suggests the `<source>` tag. Press *Tab* to complete the code. Press the *Space bar*. Type `sr`, as you do, code hinting suggests `<src>`. Then press the *Tab* key. A **Browse** link appears.

To locate a source video file, double-click on the **Browse** link provided by code hinting to open the **Select File** dialog.

Then, navigate to the h.264 video file you exported from Media Encoder into your Dreamweaver site folder. Double-click on that file to select it.

Alternate video for non-HTML5 environments

Internet Explorer 9 includes HTML5 video support. However, many folks are still watching online video in older versions of Internet Explorer—IE 8, 7, and 6. So it's important to include alternative access to online video that doesn't require HTML5 support.

To do that, you can add a line of code that provides a link to a FLV file. This line of code should be at the end of the set of parameters for the `<video>` tag, right before the `</video>` closing tag. That line of code is included in the following example.

Putting it all together

We'll walk through a step-by-step example of embedding HTML5 video at the end of this chapter that uses all the important `<video>` tag parameters, and incorporates all three HTML5 video formats, and provides accessibility for non-HTML5 browsers.

However, as a short course in that, the following lines of code display a 320 x 240 video with controls, with all three HTML5 video formats, and an option for folks with older versions of IE to watch the video as an FLV video:

```
<video width="320px" height="240px" controls>
<source src="Video/on_record.mp4">
<source src="Video/on_record.theora.ogv">
<source src="Video/on_record.webm">
<a href="Video/on_record_1.flv">Click to watch this video using Flash
Player</a>
</video>
```

Testing HTML5 video pages

It is more than clear, at this point in our exploration of HTML5 video, that presenting online video in HTML5 presents major compatibility issues. Will a video really play in the whole range of browsing environments out there, ranging from an iPad to Internet Explorer 6.0 on a Windows machine?

If you supply all three HTML5 video format options and include a link to a Flash Video page for visitors without HTML5 video support, your video should play in any environment.

Previewing a video in Live View

There are two options for testing your video in Dreamweaver. One of them, which can be found by navigating to **File | Preview in Browser**, simply opens your page in one of the browsers installed on your own computer. This is effective and useful for testing video in browsers you already have installed.

A quicker way to see if your video works, at least in Safari and other browsers that follow the Webkit standard (and this includes Apple mobile devices) is to simply look at, and test the video in **Live View**. If you are working in the **Split** view (pretty much a necessity for working with HTML5 video in Dreamweaver), you can click on the **Live View** button, and test your video even as you see (and edit) code on the code side of **Split** view.

Embedding an HTML5 video

The following example walks step-by-step through everything you need to make HTML5 video available in all three available compressed video formats, along with an option for FLV for older versions of Internet Explorer (versions 6-8).

As with all our examples in this book, the first step is to be sure you have a defined the Dreamweaver website. With that in place, create and save a page called `video.html` in the site.

The sample code here uses a real video file (NYC Sunset) that I uploaded to my Vimeo channel (search for "David Karlins"). You can use this to experiment with. If you do, download it from Vimeo by clicking on the **Download** button for the video.

Then, prepare multiple versions of the video by translating the downloaded h.264 (`nyc_sunset_424x320.mp4`) video to OGG and WebM using Micro Converter (see the *Converting video to web formats with open source tools* section in this chapter for tips on doing that).

Save the three video files in a folder called `video` within your site root folder.

With your site defined, an HTML5 page (`video.html`) saved, and with the (downloaded) mp4/h.264 video, and (converted) OGG and WebM videos in the video folder of your site, you're ready for the following steps:

1. In the Dreamweaver **Document** window, jump into **Split** view, and in the **Code** side of the **Split** view, click where you wish to create a new line of code. This can be anywhere in between the `<body>` and `</body>` tags. As we are working with a brand new document, place your cursor after the first `<body>` tag and press *Enter* (Windows) or *Return* (Mac) to create a new line of code.

2. Start typing the `<video` element. A couple of letters into the process, you can press the *Tab* key to complete the beginning of the element.

3. Add a video parameter named `controls` to display controls.

4. Close the `<video>` tag by typing > and press *Return* to create a new line of code.

5. Close the video element by typing `</video>`.

6. After the opening `video` tag, but before the closing `video` tag, define the first video source with the following line of code:

```
<source src=" nyc_sunset_424x320.mp4">
```

7. At this stage, you can see (and hear!) the video in **Live** view in the **Design** side of **Split** view, as shown in the following screenshot:

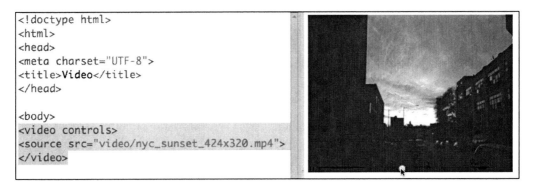

```
<!doctype html>
<html>
<head>
<meta charset="UTF-8">
<title>Video</title>
</head>

<body>
<video controls>
<source src="video/nyc_sunset_424x320.mp4">
</video>
```

8. On a new line of code, enter the HTML5 code to define the Theora OGG video as a second video source:

```
<source src="/video nyc_sunset_424x320.ogv">
```

9. You can test this second line of code by previewing your page in Google Chrome, if you have that browser installed. The current version of Chrome does not support h.264 video, so the `.mp4` file will not be recognized, but the `.ogv` (OGG) file will be.

```
Preview in Firefox              ⌥F12
Preview in Google Chrome
Preview in IE 5
Preview in Safari
Preview in Shadow
Preview in Adobe BrowserLab     ⇧⌘F12

Edit Browser List...
```

10. Add a line of code defining the third video source:

```
<source src="video/nyc_sunset_424x320.webm">
```

11. On a new line of code, simply type: `Click here to watch the video`. Select the word `here` and use the **Insert Hyperlink** dialog to define a link to `http://vimeo.com/22366228`, which opens in a new browser window (choose **_blank** from the **Target** popup).

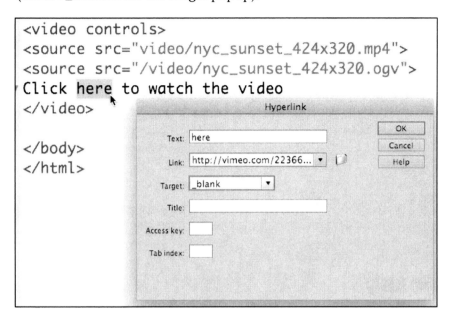

```
<video controls>
<source src="video/nyc_sunset_424x320.mp4">
<source src="/video/nyc_sunset_424x320.ogv">
Click here to watch the video
</video>

</body>
</html>
```

This last link is our "fail safe" option for users with very old browsers that do not support any HTML5 video. They can watch the video at Vimeo.

12. Feel free to touch up the page with text or styles. Or not. Save your file. If you have access to IE 6, 7, or 8, you can test the non-HTML version, or you can test that using Adobe BrowserLab (**File | Preview in Browser | Adobe BrowserLab**)

The entire code for our example project is as follows:

```
<!doctype html>

<html>

<head>

<meta charset="UTF-8">

<title>Video</title>
```

```
</head>


<body>

<video controls>

<source src="video/nyc_sunset_424x320.mp4">

<source src="/video/nyc_sunset_424x320.ogv">
<source src="/video/nyc_sunset_424x320.webm">
Click <a href="http://vimeo.com/22366228" target="_blank">here</a> to
watch the video

</video>


</body>

</html>
```

Summary

In this chapter, we explored the process of creating and presenting HTML5 audio and video. We examined the evolving, different, and competing options for compressing audio and video supported by HTML5. Moreover, we noted the need to provide a way to present our video for non-HTML5 browsing environments by creating a FLV file that will work in those pre-HTML5 browsing environments.

Then, we walked through Dreamweaver's tools for embedding an HTML5 video. Those tools are essentially code hints, which provide help in writing HTML5 <video> tags and their properties, and Live View which previews at least the Webkit (Safari) version of the video as we write code.

Beyond the limitations of Dreamweaver menu options for embedding native audio and video, we also explored using Code view to enter our own HTML5 audio and video elements.

In the next chapter, we'll see how to use media queries in Dreamweaver. With that, we'll begin to engage with what is probably the main focus of this book, and one of the most important and exciting challenges facing today's web designer: creating web pages that are attractive, inviting, and accessible in both full-sized (laptop/desktop) environments, and in mobile devices (smart phones).

6
Responsive Design with Media Queries

It is a multimedia world. People experience and interact with web content with a variety of media, ranging from large-screen projections of websites to hand-held devices. This presents specific challenges for web designers.

One of those challenges revolves around designing pages that are accessible, inviting, and functional at highly varying sizes. A page with centered content, sidebars on the left and the right, and text flowing around images may be inviting on a laptop, but a jumbled mess on an iPhone.

With the advent of HTML5 and CSS3, it is possible to design pages that detect the size of a viewing device (the viewport), and to present unique page layouts customized for that device. So, for example, you can create three alternative views of a page—one for smart phones, one for tablets, and one for full-sized monitors. The approach is referred to as **responsive design**. The CSS3 technique for implementing it is a **Media Query**.

In this chapter, we'll learn to design pages in Dreamweaver that detect media viewports using Dreamweaver-generated Media Queries, and present appropriate page designs tailored to the visitor's viewing environment.

While doing that, we will:

- Use Dreamweaver's Multiscreen Preview window to preview how sites will look in different viewports
- Customize Multiscreen Preview for specific devices
- Create multiple styles for differently sized viewing devices with Dreamweaver's Media Queries

Web design for a multimedia web world

As noted in the introduction to this chapter, recent times have seen an explosion in the variety of media through which people interact with websites, particularly the way smart phones and tablets are defining the browsing experience more and more. Moreover, as noted, a web page design that is appropriate may be necessary for a wide-screen experience but is often inappropriate, overly cluttered, or just plain dysfunctional on a tiny screen.

The solution is Media Queries—a new element of CSS stylesheets introduced with CSS3. But before we examine new media features in CSS3, it will be helpful to understand the basic evolutionary path that led to the development of CSS3 Media Queries. That background will be useful both in getting our heads around the concepts involved and because in the crazy Wild West state of browsing environments these days (with emerging and yet-unresolved standards conflicts), designing for the widest range of media requires combining new CSS3 Media Queries with older CSS Media detection tools. We'll see how this plays out in real life near the end of this chapter, when we examine particular challenges of creating Media Queries that can detect, for example, an Apple iPhone.

How Media Queries work

Let's look at an example. If you open the Boston Globe (newspaper) site (`http://www.bostonglobe.com/`) in a browser window the width of a laptop, you'll see a three-column page layout (go ahead, I'll wait while you check; or just take a look at the following example).

The three-column layout works well in laptops. But in a smaller viewport, the design adjusts to present content in two columns, as shown in the following screenshot:

The two-column layout is the same HTML page as the three-column layout. And the content of both pages (text, images, media, and so on) is the same. The crew at the Globe do not have to build a separate home page for tablets or smartphones. But a media query has linked a different CSS file that displays in narrower viewports.

A short history of Media Queries

Stepping back in time a bit, the current (pre-CSS3) version of CSS could already detect media, and enable different stylesheets depending on the media. Moreover, Dreamweaver CS6 (also CS5.5, CS5, and previous versions) provided very nice, intuitive support for these features.

The way this works in Dreamweaver is that when you click the **Attach Style Sheet** icon at the bottom of the **CSS Styles** panel (with a web page open in Dreamweaver's **Document** window), the **Attach External Style Sheet** dialog appears.

The **Media** popup in the dialog allows you to attach a stylesheet specifically designed for print, aural (to be read out loud by the reader software), Braille, handheld devices, and other "traditional" output options, as well as newer CSS3-based options. The **handheld** option, shown in the following screenshot, was available before CSS3:

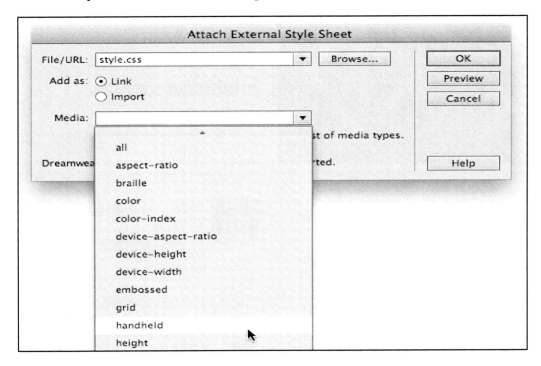

So, to summarize the evolutionary path, detecting media and providing a custom style for that media is not new to HTML5 and its companion CSS3, and there is support for those features in Dreamweaver CS6. Detecting and synchronizing styles with defined media has been available in Dreamweaver.

However, what is relatively new is the ability to detect and supply defined stylesheets for specific screen sizes. And that new feature opens the door to new levels of customized page design for specific media.

HTML5, CSS3, and Media Queries

With HTML5 and CSS3, Media Queries have been expanded. We can now define all kinds of criteria for selecting a stylesheet to apply to a viewing environment, including orientation (whether or not a mobile phone, tablet, and so on, is held in the portrait [up-down] or landscape [sideways] view), whether the device displays color, the shape of the viewing area, and — of most value — the width and height of the viewing area.

All these options present a multitude of possibilities for creating custom stylesheets for different viewing environments. In fact they open up a ridiculously large array of possibilities. But for most designers, simply creating three appropriate stylesheets, one for laptop/desktop viewing, one for mobile phones, and one for tablets, is sufficient.

In order to define criteria for which stylesheet will display in an environment, HTML5 and CSS3 allow us to use `if-then` statements. So, for example, if we are assigning a stylesheet to tablets, we might specify that if the width of the viewing area is greater than that of a cell phone, but smaller than that of a laptop screen, we want the tablet stylesheet to be applied.

Styling for mobile devices and tablets

While a full exploration of the aesthetic dimensions of creating styles for different media is beyond the scope of our mission in this book, it is worth noting a few basic "dos and don'ts" vis-à-vis styling for mobile devices.

I'll be back with more detailed advice on mobile styling later in this chapter, but in a word, the challenge is: simplify. In general, this means applying many or all of the following adjustments to your pages:

- Smaller margins
- Larger (more readable) type
- Much less complex backgrounds; no image backgrounds
- No sidebars or floated content (content around which other content wraps)
- Often, no containers that define page width

 Design advice online: If you search for "css for mobile devices" online, you'll find thousands of articles with different perspectives and advice on designing web pages that can be easily accessed with handheld devices.

Media Queries versus jQuery Mobile and apps

Before moving to the technical dimension of building pages with responsive design using Media Queries, let me briefly compare and contrast media queries to the two other options available for displaying content differently for fullscreen and mobile devices.

One option is an **app**. Apps (short for applications) are full-blown computer programs created in a high-level programming language. Dreamweaver CS6 includes new tools to connect with and generate apps through the online PhoneGap resources. We cover that process in some depth in the final chapter of this book, *Chapter 10, Building Apps with PhoneGap*.

The second option is a jQuery Mobile site. jQuery Mobile sites are based on JavaScript. But, as we'll see later in this book, you don't need to know JavaScript to build jQuery Mobile sites. The main difference between jQuery Mobile sites and Media Query sites with mobile-friendly designs is that jQuery Mobile sites require different content while Media Query sites simply repackage the same content with different stylesheets.

Which approach should you use, Media Queries or JavaScript? That is a judgment call. What I can advise here is that Media Queries provides the easiest way to create and maintain a mobile version of your site.

Previewing with Multiscreen Preview

Dreamweaver's Multiscreen Preview provides an instant (if not precise) preview of how a web page will look in the three different viewing environments.

To view an open web page in **Multiscreen Preview**, go to **View | Toolbars | Document**, or go to **Window | Multiscreen Preview** from the **Document** window menu. When you do, the **Multiscreen Preview** window opens, with three views, as shown in the following screenshot:

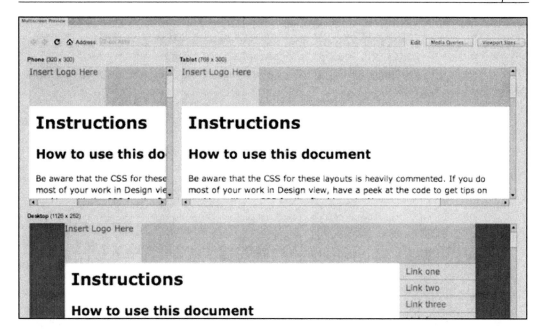

Multiscreen Preview is a form of Live view. You can't edit content there, you can only preview how a page will look in a browser. You can, however—as we shall see—edit the stylesheets associated with each view, and observe the effect in Multiscreen Preview.

The three preset viewport sizes in the **Multiscreen Preview** window provide a pretty widely applicable set of screen sizes for previewing how an open page will look in a smartphone, a tablet, and on a desktop (or a full-sized laptop with a screen width of 1024 pixels or more). The width settings are a good, general way to preview how your page will look in different media.

On the other hand, if you are designing for a specific viewing environment, you can customize these settings. To do that, click on the **Viewport Sizes** button in the upper-right corner of the **Multiscreen Preview** window. That opens the **Viewport Sizes** dialog. You can change the width (and, in the case of phones and tablets, the height) of any of the three available views by changing the values in the **Width** or **Height** box, and clicking on **OK**.

The most useful adjustment you make in **Viewport Sizes** dialog might actually be the height of the **Phone** preview. By making that value a bit larger, you can get more of a sense of how pages will look in smartphones with longer viewing screens. In the following screenshot, the height of the **Phone** preview window is being changed to **480** pixels:

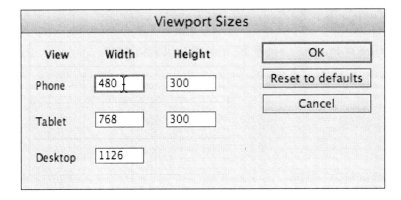

When you first preview a page, you will most probably not like the way it looks in the phone and tablet preview windows. At that point, you can do one of two things, as follows:

- Elect not to worry about how the page looks and works in mobile devices, under the assumption that this mobile device thing is a passing fad that will soon go away
- You can use Dreamweaver to generate a Media Query to present more inviting, accessible content in mobile devices

Assuming you chose the latter, let's move on to explore how to create stylesheets for phone and tablet display, and to apply these stylesheets in the appropriate environments.

Generating a Media Query in Dreamweaver CS6

There are a number of valid approaches and possible protocols you can use to generate the sets of styles for a Media Query in Dreamweaver CS6. Before walking through one that works well, let's survey what it is we're trying to accomplish.

Dreamweaver's tools for creating Media Queries in CS6 are a bit enhanced compared to those in Dreamweaver CS5.5; therefore, readers using older versions of Dreamweaver will find a few of the options we explore below unavailable.

Essentially, we need three sets of stylesheets—one for phones, one for tablets, and one for full-sized monitors. Because full-sized monitors are still, at this point, a "standard" in terms of how web content is viewed, and because the phone and tablet styles will likely have less complex styles, it makes sense to start by creating a stylesheet for a full-sized page.

In other words, the first step is to create a basic CSS stylesheet that works well with the page when it is opened in a full-sized desktop or laptop monitor. Then, variations on that page can be generated with simplified layouts that work on phones and tablets.

Building alternative stylesheets

As noted, from a style and accessibility perspective, it makes sense to start with a "full-sized" web page style and then build permutations of that style that work with phones and tablets.

There is also a technical reason to use that workflow. Keep in mind that all three CSS stylesheet files will be providing styling rules for the same page. That means all three alternative CSS files have to provide rules for the same set of HTML elements and tags.

For example, if a `<div>` tag defines a main container on a page, the stylesheets for all three media (phone, tablet, and desktop) have to define how that `<div>` tag should appear. The rules for the phone CSS might include a narrower width, a simpler background color, and other attributes. But, the point is that all three stylesheets will have rules for this main container `div` tag. And that must be the case for all the layout elements, whether HTML5 layout elements, `<div>` tags, or some combination of the two.

Preparing to generate a Media Query

One effective protocol for preparing to generate a Media Query is to have three CSS files ready to assign to different media.

A simple protocol for doing that is as follows:

1. Create a basic CSS file for your page that works for desktop- or laptop-sized monitors. If you are generating pages from Dreamweaver CS6's HTML5 layouts, you can use the CSS file that comes with the respective layout as this "main" layout.

2. Save the "main" CSS file with a filename such as `full-size.css` and then resave it twice with two different filenames (such as `tablet.css` and `smartphone.css`), creating three identical stylesheets. Alternately, if you only want to provide two options (and let tablet users see the full-size styles), just save two versions of the CSS file—`full-size.css` and `smartphone.css`.

3. With the alternative stylesheets saved, you can customize them right in the **Multiscreen Preview** menu.

With three alternative CSS files available for assignment and editing, you're ready to define Media Queries. We'll walk through that process next.

Assigning styles to different media

The best way to avail oneself of Dreamweaver's tools for building Media Queries is to work in the Multiscreen Preview mode. Remember, this means we will not be editing content as we adjust styles. But that constraint is something we can definitely live with, and in fact, as a general approach, adjusting content and style should be thought of and approached as distinct processes.

So, our scenario is that we've opened **Multiscreen Preview** for an open web page. And we have at the ready three different CSS files—the ones discussed in the "3-step" protocol identified just a bit earlier in this chapter.

With at least two CSS files saved as part of your Dreamweaver site, and with a web page open in **Multiscreen Preview**, follow these steps to define custom styles for each view:

1. Click on the **Media Queries** button to open the **Media Queries** dialog.

2. In the **Write Media Queries To** area, choose the **This Document** option. The **Site-Wide Media Query File** alternative is trickier; it involves Dreamweaver changing code in all your pages and is less reliable.

3. Leave the **Force Devices to Report Actual Width** checkbox selected. This overcomes any confusion that can be caused when different devices define "pixels" in ways that distort their actual width. The initial selections in the **Media Queries** dialog should look like the following:

```
                        Media Queries

Media Queries let you target your designs for multiple devices by specifying a different CSS file for
each device.

   Write media queries to:

        ○  Site-wide media query file:    [ Specify... ]

            The changes you make in this dialog will affect all other pages that include the
            site-wide media queries file. You can select which file to use for this in the
            Advanced Settings section of the Site Setup dialog.

        ◉  This document


   ☑  Force devices to report actual width

        Inserting a special meta tag in your document will force certain devices to report
        their actual width instead of reporting a false width and then scaling the page.
```

4. Click on the **+** icon to add a stylesheet. The **Properties** area becomes active for that selected stylesheet:

   ° In the **Description** field, enter text that describes the style (this is for your own benefit, not for public display).

   ° In the **Min Width** field, enter a value that defines the narrowest viewport in which this style will display, wherever that is appropriate. If you are defining a CSS style for smartphones, you would not have any minimum width as that style would apply no matter how small the viewport.

   ° In the **Max Width** field, enter a value that defines the narrowest viewport in which this style will display, wherever that is appropriate. If you are defining a CSS style for full-size browsers, you would not have any maximum width as that style would apply no matter how large the viewport.

○ Use the **Select File** icon in the **CSS File** area to navigate to and select a stylesheet file that will apply in viewports that meet the defined criteria, as shown in the following screenshot:

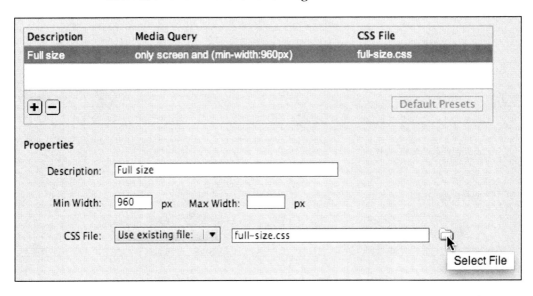

5. Repeat step 4 to add additional stylesheets to the media query. All the associated styles will be listed as shown in the following screenshot:

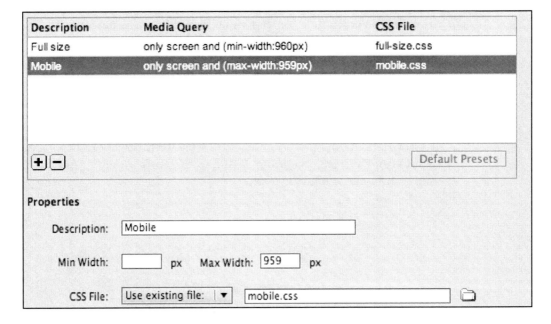

6. Click **OK** to close the **Media Queries** dialog, and see your media query applied in the **Multiscreen Preview** window as shown here:

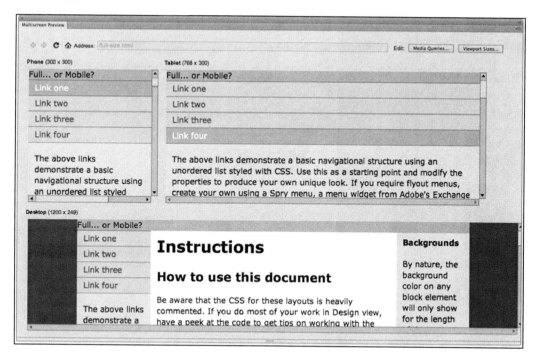

7. At any point, you can toggle in or out of **Multiscreen Preview** by choosing **Multiscreen Preview** from the **Window** menu.

Formatting CSS files for Media Queries

With a Media Query defined for a web page, we can interactively create and adjust the styles for each targeted browsing environment. To do that, re-open the Multiscreen Preview for the page.

"Wait!", you might exclaim, "how can I edit the page in Multiscreen Preview when that window functions like Live view in the Document window—locking out any content editing?". A thoughtful concern, but here we will be only editing the CSS styles, not the page content. And that we can do in **Multiscreen Preview**.

To edit styles in **Multiscreen Preview**, view the **CSS Styles** panel (**Window | CSS Styles**). The attached styles, along with the parenthetical notes that help us remember which style is which, appear in the top-half of the **CSS Styles** panel.

You can expand any of those styles by clicking the triangle next to the style's name in the top-half of the **CSS Styles** panel. In the following screenshot, the `mobile.css` style is expanded. And clicking on a style rule within the style (in this case, the `font` parameter of the `body` tag style) reveals the parameters for that style in the bottom-half of the **CSS Styles** panel.

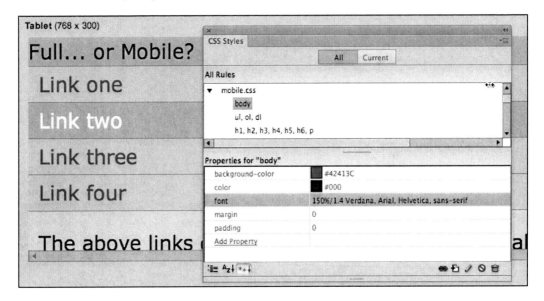

Adjusting CSS for Mobile

As pointed out earlier, the art of designing styles for mobile devices is, well, an art. And, as suggested earlier, there are tons of online resources opining and advising on what to include in phone and tablet styles. But before highlighting a few widely agreed-on elements of mobile-device styling, it is important to issue a warning: don't delete style rules from any of your stylesheet files.

Our protocol for creating the three alternative stylesheets for a Media Query started with one stylesheet, from which we created two copies. Those stylesheets "came into the world" with identical sets of style rules.

It is fine and necessary to change the parameters of those style rules. You can have different formatting for containers, text, backgrounds, and so on, in your phone style than you have in your tablet style. No problem. But keep in mind that all three of your styles have to mesh with the same HTML file, with the same CSS style names used to define formatting and layout tags and elements.

As for styling mobile devices, the following techniques are widely applicable:

- Keep the type large.
- Keep links easy to find. Underlined links are passé in full-sized web pages, but helpful on cell phones.
- Use nice large margins and/or padding in containers to make it easy for big stubby fingers to select tiny content on cell phone screens.
- Avoid sidebars (don't use the `float` attribute).
- Use `visibility: hidden` to hide non-essential elements in phone styles. In the following screenshot, `visibility` has been set to `hidden` for the header in the phone style, and the height of the header has been reduced to 1 pixel so as to create a thin line of spacing for aesthetic reasons and so it does not occupy precious space on a smart phone screen.

The following screenshot shows three stylesheets applied to the same page in **Multiscreen Preview**. The tablet view only required a few adjustments—basically reducing the widths of the layout elements (the main container, the sidebar, and the header). The phone stylesheet took more trial-and-error experimentation, including removing all `float` attributes and reducing the width of different elements. Different color schemes were applied to each stylesheet as well, with a very basic color scheme (black and white) applied to the cell phone style.

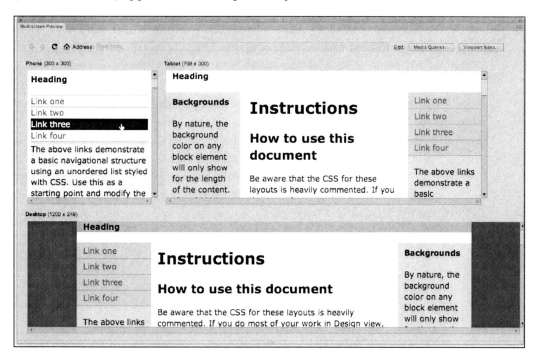

As they say in the commercials for weight-loss products, "your results may vary." Meaning, tweaking a stylesheet for a phone does require some trial and error. But again, the basic rule is: simpler. Eliminating floats (so no content appears in a second column) is usually the first step.

Defining a Media Query for smartphones

In this example, we'll walk through, step by step, how to use Dreamweaver's flexible and highly useful three-column HTML5 layout. We will create a Media Query to display this two-column content in a layout more appropriate for cell phones—without columns or sidebars.

As always, the starting assumption is that you are working in a Dreamweaver site (refer back to *Chapter 1, Creating Sites and Pages with Dreamweaver CS6*, if that doesn't register). With a site defined, the following steps will produce a nice, appropriately minimalist layout for your page in a cell phone:

1. Go to **File | New**. In the **New Document** dialog, select the **Blank Page** category. Choose **HTML** from the **Page Type** column, and choose the first HTML5 layout, **2 column fixed, centered**, from the **Layout** column. In the **New Document** dialog, leave the **Layout CSS** pop-up selection at **Create New File**. Make sure there are no files selected in the **Attach CSS File** box (if there are, use the **Trashcan** icon to delete them). With these settings in place, click **Create**.

2. The **Save Style Sheet File As** dialog opens. Change the saved stylesheet name to `fullsize.css`, and click **Save** to save the stylesheet to your site's folder.

3. The web page opens in the Dreamweaver **Document** window. Let's make two edits to the content:
   - Delete the `http://www.adobe.com/go/adc_css_layouts` link. That link is inappropriately long, particularly for a cell phone. If (in real life) we wanted to link to a site with a long URL, we could assign the link to much shorter text by going to **Insert | Hyperlink**.
   - In the header area, type `Full...` or `Mobile?`.

4. Go to **File | Save** to save the edited HTML page as `2_views.html`.

5. Next, we will create a CSS file to build from to display content in a mobile device. Go to **File | New**. In the **New Document** dialog, choose **CSS** from the **Page Type** list and click on the **Create** button. Go to **File | Save**, and save the new, blank CSS file as `mobile.css`. Copy and paste all the code in the original `fullsize.css` file into the new `mobile.css` file. We'll edit these styles next.

6. Return to the `2_views.html` page in the **Document** window. You can do that either by clicking on the file in the **Files** tab bar at the top of the **Document** window, or by using the **Window** menu.

7. Go to **Window | Multiscreen Preview**; click on the **Media Queries** button in **Multiscreen Preview** to open the **Media Queries** dialog.

8. For tablets and full-sized computers, for the sake of this example, we will simply display the already attached CSS file (`fullsize.css`). Click on the + icon to add a stylesheet. The **Properties** area becomes active for the new stylesheet:

   ○ In the **Description** field, enter `Full Size`.

   ○ In the **Min Width** field, enter `960`. This style will only apply to viewports with a width of at least 960 pixels.

   ○ Leave the **Max Width** field blank. As we are defining a CSS style for full-sized browsers, we do not want to set a maximum width; this style will be applied no matter how wide the viewport.

   ○ Use the **Select File** icon in the **CSS File** area to navigate to and select the `fullsize.css` stylesheet file that will apply in viewports that meet the defined criteria.

9. For smartphones, we will display the `mobile.css` file we created in the fifth step. Click on the **+** icon to add a stylesheet. The **Properties** area becomes active for the new stylesheet.

   ○ In the **Description** field, enter `Mobile`.

   ○ Leave the **Min Width** field blank. This style will apply to viewports with width less than 960 pixels.

   ○ In the **Max Width** field, enter `960`. As we are defining a CSS style for mobile phones, we do not want this stylesheet to display in viewports wider than 960 pixels.

   ○ Use the **Select File** icon in the **CSS File** area to navigate to and select the `mobile.css` stylesheet file that will apply in viewports that meet the defined criteria.

10. View the page layouts in **Multiscreen Preview**; the layout for the full screen viewport is not bad. But the page layout and colors won't work well in mobile devices. Let's make some adjustments in the mobile version of the page, as follows:

   ° Change the font size for the body tag to 150%, providing larger text for mobile devices, as shown here:

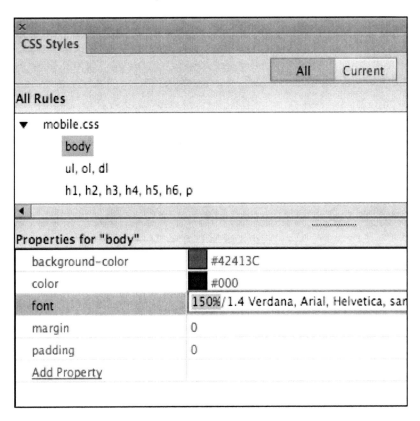

   ° We want to remove all width and float parameters in every style rule for our mobile style. Those width and float parameters create columns, and content that doesn't fill the entire width of the page, and make the display in a mobile phone inaccessible and uninviting. Go through each of the styles in the mobile.css stylesheet and click to left of every width or float parameter to convert that code to comments, as shown here:

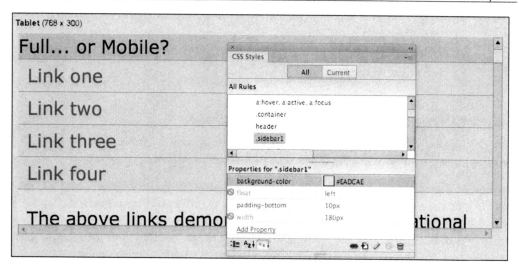

° Consider adjusting the color scheme to create a higher contrast between background and foreground colors, to make the page easier to read and navigate in different lighting conditions encountered by mobile phone users (including bright, outdoor, and sunlight). The following example shows higher contrast assigned to the navigation element:

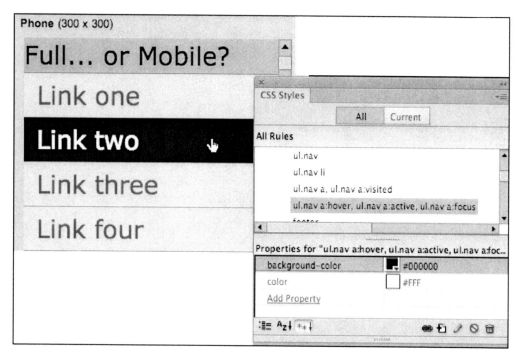

11. That's it! There's more tweaking we could do, but remember that when designing for mobile devices, less really is more. Exit **Multiscreen Preview** (go to **Window | Multiscreen Preview** to deselect this view). Save your page with changes to the CSS.

Surveying alternative approaches

In this chapter, we focused on creating media queries using Dreamweaver's **Multiscreen Preview** window and **Media Queries** dialog box.

Another approach to defining Media Queries is to create them within a single CSS file. The advantage of this approach is that styles for all viewports are in the same CSS file. The disadvantage is that this makes CSS files two, three, or even four (or more) times as long, bulky, and hard to edit. On the balance, I would argue that in most situations the approach we've taken so far is easier to manage, but since Dreamweaver includes a substantial template that uses the single-CSS file approach, let's survey how this works.

The syntax to define a Media Query within a CSS file is:

```
@media only screen and (value)
```

The value can include a max-width, a min-width, or both.

In this example, the background color for the body tag is yellow for viewports of 480 pixels or less, and green for viewports of 481 pixels or more:

```
@media only screen and (max-width: 480px)
{

body {
  background-color: yellow;}

}


@media only screen and (min-width: 481px)

{

body {
  background-color: green;
}

}
```

As I pointed out, Dreamweaver CS6 includes a substantial and complex sample page that includes CSS files with Media Queries for multiple viewports within the same CSS files, and JavaScripting as well.

Again, Dreamweaver's Fluid Grid layout is one specific (and complex) sample, for example, of a Media Query using the technique of defining styles for multiple viewports within a single CSS file.

As with all Dreamweaver sample pages, you can use this page for education and inspiration; it is well documented (except for JavaScript). If you're interested in examining this sample, go to **File | New Fluid Grid Layout** and explore the options in the **New Document** dialog box for this page sample.

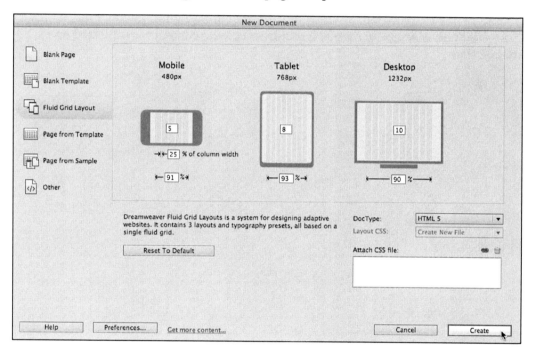

Summary

Older versions of HTML and CSS allowed for Media Queries to identify output devices including printers, Braille readers, and audio-reader devices. New additions in CSS3 allow Media Queries to detect screen size (in pixels) as well as other more esoteric properties of a browsing environment.

Dreamweaver CS6's Multiscreen preview and Media Queries dialog work together to preview and edit how the same HTML page content will display differently in a smart phone, a tablet, and a full-sized monitor.

In the next chapter of this book, we'll begin to explore a different approach to creating mobile-friendly sites: jQuery Mobile. The jQuery Mobile approach provides a more dynamic, animated, inviting style for mobile sites, but, as you'll see in *Chapter 7, Mobile Pages with jQuery Mobile*, it requires separate content for full-sized and mobile sites.

7
Creating Mobile Pages with jQuery Mobile

As a web design consultant, I'm immersed for periods of time studying statistical trends—who is using the Web? To do what? In what browsing environments? But you probably don't need a summary of my research to know that both in numbers and in impact, people using mobile devices constitute the dynamic factor in web activity. I'll share one statistic compiled from a number of surveys I've been sifting through: as this edition of our book goes to press, about half of all visits to websites will be from mobile devices. And in categories such as entertainment and restaurants, an overwhelming amount of web browsing is already done using mobile devices.

Are they using web browsers for this? Or apps? Both. But at this stage of the game, mobile websites provide a far more accessible technique for developers. You can, and will, create fully mobile-friendly websites with jQuery Mobile that look and feel like apps but that do not require the high-level coding involved in building apps.

This is not our first engagement with the challenges of designing for multiple media. In *Chapter 6, Responsive Design with Media Queries*, we began by exploring pages built with HTML5's Media Queries to present the same content, but with different styling, for full-sized, mobile, and tablet-sized pages. And in *Chapter 5, Embedding Native Audio and Video*, we explored using HTML5 audio and video to embed mobile-friendly (non-Flash) video in web pages.

jQuery Mobile pages provide a more radical approach to creating mobile-friendly content than simply using Media Queries and mobile-friendly video. jQuery Mobile pages involve creating *different, distinct* content for mobile devices (usually shorter, more compressed content) and presenting that content in a radically different way from websites aimed at desktop and laptop users. We'll explore what that means next.

The following topics are covered in this chapter:

- Design for mobile—an overview
- Apps and mobile pages
- The three components of Mobile Web: HTML5, CSS, and jQuery Mobile
- jQuery Mobile in Dreamweaver
- Generating mobile-ready pages from starter pages
- Customizing Mobile starter page content
- Adding "pages"
- Customizing mobile page CSS

Mobile pages – an overview

The principles involved with designing mobile sites can be boiled down to one word: simple.

Mobile sites have to be simple in design. People are viewing and interacting with them on small devices. It is for this reason that columns, sidebars, and complex backgrounds that work well on a laptop or desktop are uninviting and inaccessible on mobile devices.

The second dimension of "simple" when it comes to design for mobile devices is that sites can't be loaded up with plugins (such as Flash), server-side scripting (such as PHP), or complicated navigation schemes. Some of these features are supported in some mobile devices (Flash is supported in some versions of the Android operating system), but most are not. Moreover, mobile devices have limited processing power, battery time, and other constraints that take us back to the watchword: simple.

Laptops and desktops on one hand and mobile devices on the other have quite different interface features. Obviously, in most cases, desktop/laptop viewports (screens) are wider. So multicolumn page layouts are not only possible, they are generally necessary to present inviting content. This is not the case with mobile phones and not even with large tablets.

Desktop and laptop computers have a mouse or some kind of hover device that can hover over an object; mobile devices have touchscreens that can be resized or scrolled.

Take some time to examine your favorite sites on both a full-sized viewport and in a mobile device. You'll see that professionally designed sites have a separate mobile presence that takes these factors into account. YouTube, for example, presents a multicolumn grid in a laptop and takes advantage of hovering to allow users to get pop-up content when they hover over an element on the page.

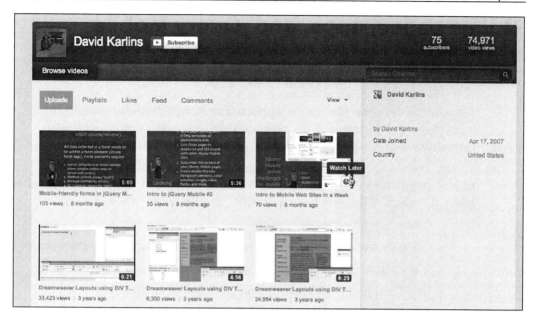

On the other hand, if you visit YouTube on an iPhone, you'll experience a
single-column site that does not rely on hovering.

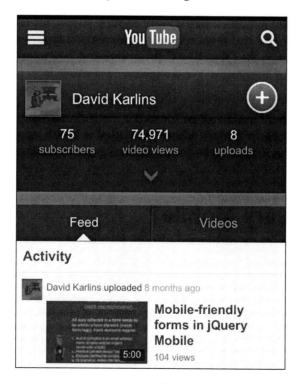

Mobile pages, apps, and jQuery Mobile

In the introduction to this chapter, I briefly pointed out the relationship between using responsive design (Media Queries), jQuery Mobile, and apps to present mobile-accessible pages. Let me expand on that a bit:

- Responsive design is the easiest approach to mobile-friendly content from a development perspective because with this approach you use the same content for all your pages and simply present distinct page layouts.

- jQuery Mobile requires more work since it involves distinct content for mobile pages, different from that provided to fullscreen visitors. On the other hand, jQuery Mobile sites have a number of advantages such as:

  ○ They download more quickly

  ○ They provide inviting animation and interactivity for mobile users

  ○ They allow the use of special, mobile-friendly navigation elements

  ○ They enable form elements that work better in small screens.

 The remainder of this chapter will walk you through how that works

- Apps look and act much like jQuery Mobile pages but require a whole other level of expertise and resources for their creation and maintenance. Apps are written either in the Objective-C programming language or in other complex programming languages. We'll explore PhoneGap in depth in the last chapter of this book.

While app development makes sense for major institutions with relatively unlimited development resources, or people whose main goal is to sell apps for profit at iTunes, an overwhelming majority of websites are served best with either responsive design or jQuery Mobile.

What is jQuery Mobile?

jQuery is a library of JavaScript-based objects. JavaScript works in any browser or operating system. It is an open source (free) software.

OK, so what is JavaScript? And what is a library?

JavaScript is a *client-side* scripting language. That is, it is a programming language that creates animation and interactivity that is run in browsers ("client" is more or less a techie term for browser). Another way to put it: JavaScript (almost always) runs on a user's computer, not on a server.

JavaScript has been part of Dreamweaver for as as long as Dreamweaver has existed. The rather abandoned **Behaviors** panel generates JavaScript. Spry widgets (introduced in the earlier versions of Dreamweaver) are JavaScript based. In another dimension of web design, that is, outside of Dreamweaver, jQuery has evolved as a relatively accessible set of customizable JavaScript objects. Now when I say relatively accessible, I mean that implementing JavaScript through the jQuery library still requires editing JavaScript code.

A library, in the context in which we're using the word here, is usually a combination of HTML, CSS, and a programming language. What you get from such libraries are sets of files: one or more HTML files, one or more CSS files, and one or more program files that add animation and interactivity to HTML and CSS. These files work together—you need HTML, CSS, and the program script to make the library element work.

With the emergence of mobile devices, a distinct JavaScript library emerged—jQuery Mobile—with a set of objects particularly useful in designing for mobile devices.

Creating mobile pages from Dreamweaver starters

A small, but very substantial, set of jQuery Mobile objects are available in the **Design** view in Dreamweaver. They don't require coding! The most widely used of these objects have been bundled into a very handy set of customizable starter pages. In this chapter, we'll create pages using these starters, examine them, and customize the HTML and CSS that control the content and look of these pages.

The jQuery objects that come with mobile starter pages in Dreamweaver are not customizable themselves. In this way, they differ a bit from the Spry widgets in Dreamweaver where you can often customize some of the JavaScript itself. But as we'll see, this isn't going to be much of a problem because you can do most of the customizing you can imagine doing by editing the HTML and CSS associated with jQuery Mobile objects.

How does that work? Dreamweaver has set up tools that allow us to customize jQuery Mobile objects without worrying about what is happening under the surface. But as a very basic foundation, it is helpful to understand that JavaScript (and this applies to both Spry and jQuery Mobile objects) works either on HTML objects (such as tags, often including `div` tags) or on defined CSS style properties.

For example, a jQuery object might change its background color when clicked (or tapped on a mobile device). But the colors—both before and after—are defined in an associated CSS rule that is accessible in the **CSS Styles** panel. Moreover, the content (text, images, media) in that object is defined by the HTML you create in Dreamweaver's **Design** view.

Dreamweaver comes with three starter pages based on jQuery Mobile: **jQuery Mobile (CDN)**, **jQuery Mobile (Local)**, and **jQuery Mobile with theme (Local)**. You can access these options to open the **New Document** dialog by navigating to **File | New** and choosing **Page** from **Sample** in the left-hand side column and from **Mobile Starters** in the **Sample Folder** column.

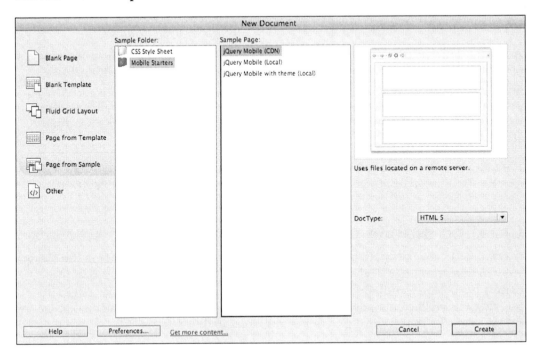

What are those three options for jQuery Mobile sample pages?

- **jQuery Mobile (CDN)** uses versions of the JavaScript and CSS that are stored and distributed through a **Central Distribution Network** (CDN) dedicated to providing jQuery Mobile. This is the most reliable and stable way to build pages in jQuery Mobile because the centrally distributed files can't be corrupted by anything you do. Furthermore, as new versions of the JavaScript and CSS files are introduced, you can update the links to them. The downside is that you can't work on your jQuery Mobile site in Dreamweaver unless you are online.

- **jQuery Mobile (Local)** uses the versions of JavaScript and CSS that come with Dreamweaver. These files are easier to corrupt as they are stored on your computer (and uploaded to your server). But you can use them to develop jQuery Mobile sites in Dreamweaver in situations where you don't have Internet access.

- The **jQuery Mobile with theme (Local)** option is new to Dreamweaver CS6 and is an attempt by Adobe to make it easier to edit the theme for a jQuery Mobile site. A theme is the portion of the required CSS that defines fonts, colors, and other styling options. My experience has been that it is easy and reliable to use one of the other options, and you can avoid this option. But we'll return to these issues in *Chapter 9, Customizing Themes with ThemeRoller*, when we explore customizing themes in detail.

 In most cases, use the **jQuery Mobile (CDN)** option to begin creating a new jQuery Mobile site.

After you click on the **Create** button in the **New Document** dialog, a web page based on jQuery Mobile opens in the Dreamweaver **Document** window.

Mobile pages in Split view

Editing and previewing jQuery Mobile pages presents a specific challenge: you cannot really see how the pages will look without going into Live view because the jQuery Mobile application that makes the page work is not displayed with the Live view. But on the other hand, you can't edit the content of a jQuery Mobile page in the Design view with the Live view on.

There are two options for handling this challenge:

- You can toggle back and forth within the **Live** view, turning it off (to edit your page) or on (to see your page)
- You can leave the **Live** view on in the **Design** window and edit it in the **Code** view

In this book, we'll use and combine both the techniques. To do this, you will find it most useful to examine the page in Split view for two reasons. In the Split view, you can both examine HTML code and see the page previewed as it will appear in a browser. Plus you can see your page in a narrower preview window that will more closely simulate how your page will look in a mobile device.

It's particularly useful while designing for mobile devices to avail yourself of the **Window Size** pop up at the bottom of the **Design** half of the **Split** view, and change the size of the **Preview** window to 480 pixels wide—a dimension that corresponds to many popular mobile devices. Do this using the **Window Size** pop-up in Dreamweaver's (bottom) status bar.

Alternatively, you can use the preset sizing buttons in the status bar for mobile-, tablet-, or desktop-sized windows:

Previewing jQuery Mobile pages in Live view

As you explore the template page generated by any of the jQuery Mobile starter pages, you'll note one thing right away that is very different from other pages you've worked with in Dreamweaver; until you flip on the Live view (click on the **Live View** button in the **Document** toolbar), hardly any of the formatting is visible. Try toggling it back and forth, turning **Live View** on and off to see what is and is not displayed with **Live View** off.

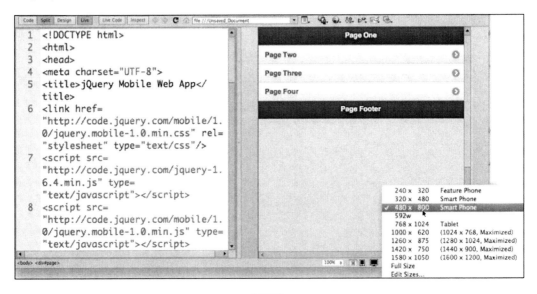

Customizing Mobile page content

In a basic sense, you customize jQuery Mobile page content the same way you customize any starter-page-generated content. Starter pages come with template content, and you can replace that with your own real content.

Simple enough? Kind of. As we've noted, there is a different order of gaps between the content and layout in jQuery Mobile pages. To put it another way, nothing is even close to how it appears with Live View turned off. And yet, you can't edit content in Live View.

The HTML5 data-role property

Div tags associated with the jQuery Mobile script can function as different kinds of elements, including ones that appear to be and act like pages in a mobile device. This is done by implementing the data-role property in HTML5 tags, and then defining CSS (stylesheet) rules to go with each data-role.

Typically, and this is the case for the starter pages in Dreamweaver, jQuery Mobile pages are organized and laid out using the following four data-roles:

- Page
- Header
- Content
- Footer

Data-role pages

The basic framework for organizing page content within an HTML page is div tags with properties of data-role-page. In other words, within a single HTML page there are usually multiple "pages" created using data-role of div tags.

You can see how this works if you take a look at both the code and page layout generated from a Dreamweaver jQuery Mobile starter. You'll see that what appears to be a "page" in Live view is actually a `div data-role` page:

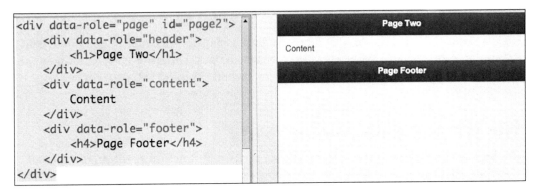

```
<div data-role="page" id="page2">
    <div data-role="header">
        <h1>Page Two</h1>
    </div>
    <div data-role="content">
        Content
    </div>
    <div data-role="footer">
        <h4>Page Footer</h4>
    </div>
</div>
```

Organizing content into what are actually `div` tags with an HTML5 property called `data-role` allows people to navigate through what feel and act like web pages. But these `div` tags, acting like pages, allow visitors to hop back and forth between "pages" without having to wait for a new page to load in their browser. The use of such `data-page` `div` tags is central to how the tiny space on a mobile device can be best used to present a lot of content.

People navigate between `data-role` pages in mobile devices by tapping, dragging, or otherwise navigating in a way that essentially shows or hides different "pages". You can familiarize yourself with how this works by navigating around the "pages" in a jQuery Mobile starter page in Live View. Use the **Back** button in the Dreamweaver **Document** window toolbar to simulate the **Back** button in a mobile browsing device:

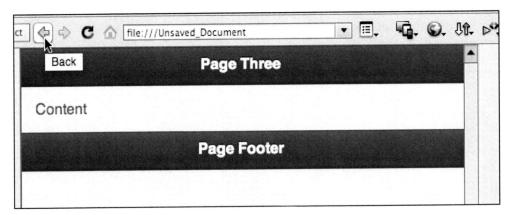

Customizing page content

Now that you understand how jQuery Mobile pages are organized and function within an HTML page, customizing the content of the "pages" in the starter page will flow pretty naturally. One way to approach this process is to kind of ignore everything else and simply replace the content in jQuery "pages" with your own content. Then, try the content out in Live View, see how it flows, and edit, move, break up, and revise the content as necessary.

Use your own content to replace the header, content, and footer for each page. Identify this code in each generated page:

```
<div data-role="page" id="page2">

  <div data-role="header">

    <h1>Page Two</h1>

  </div>
  <div data-role="content">

    Content

</div>

<div data-role="footer">

    <h4>Page Footer</h4>

  </div>

</div>
```

Replace the content in the highlighted lines of code with any HTML5 content.

> **Remember**: Use only HTML5 content in your jQuery Mobile pages. Avoid plugins such as Flash. Also, avoid server-side include content—data served into a page using server-side scripting—if that is something you work with. Server-side live data is not something we'll explore in this book, but if you are using PHP scripting, that won't fly in jQuery Mobile pages. Again, the basic rule is: stick to HTML, CSS, and JavaScript content.

Moreover, while I'm an advocate of maximizing the use of the Design view in Dreamweaver, in part because of the great gap between the content and formatting in jQuery Mobile pages, I have to confess that I generally resort to creating HTML content in the Code side of the Split view, with the Live View turned on in the Design side.

Customizing content for different data roles

Generally speaking, the process of customizing content for "pages" will consist of going through and customizing the header, content, and footer sections of the pages.

jQuery Mobile pages also use the `listview` data role to organize sets of links. Those links are—again, generally speaking—links within the HTML page to other data-role "pages". In more conventional HTML terms, these are links to named anchors. You can see how these are set up by examining the default set of (internal) listview links that come with the starter page. As you'll see, by default, they link to `#page2`, `#page3`, and `#page4`; you can copy and paste these links to create more links to more "pages". We'll explore that process in detail next.

Adding new jQuery Mobile pages and objects

The jQuery Mobile starter page comes with four pages, and links to four pages. A nice number, but what if you want to have five, or six, or seven pages?

If you need to add more "pages", copy, paste, and slightly edit (change the page numbers) the fairly easily recognizable sections of HTML code that define each "page". As you customize the content, toggle Live View on and off to see how the page will look in a browser, or as an app, using the **Window Size** pop up to define the preview environment.

Here are the things you need to do as you copy and paste to create new pages:

Copy and paste a link in the list at the top of the page and change xxx. So, for example, when you create a fifth page, that code will be added to the list after the fourth page as follows:

```
<li><a href="#page4">Page Four</a></li>

    <li><a href="#page5">Page Five</a></li>
```

As you can see, there are two changes in the copied code in the list.

You need to create a new page by copying and pasting the generated `page4` and making a `page5`. Select and copy the code that defines `page4`.

```
<div data-role="page" id="page4">
    <div data-role="header">
        <h1>Page Four</h1>
    </div>
    <div data-role="content">
        Content
    </div>
    <div data-role="footer">
        <h4>Page Footer</h4>
    </div>
</div>
```

Then paste that code after the closing `</div>` tag at the end of the **data-role** property for **page4**. Change the `id` value to `page5`.

Obviously, you will want to create custom content in the header, content, and footer sections of your new page. But in order for the link you created in the list at the top of the page to work, you also need to be sure to change the page ID to match the `href` link you defined in the list at the top of the page.

```
<div data-role="page" id="page5">
    <div data-role="header">
        <h1>Page Four</h1>
    </div>
    <div data-role="content">
        Content
    </div>
    <div data-role="footer">
        <h4>Page Footer</h4>
    </div>
</div>
```

Dreamweaver has a menu option for adding a new page. To use that, navigate to **Insert | jQuery Mobile | Page**. The **jQuery Mobile Page** dialog appears, with a preset prompt to add a page following your last existing page. The checkbox options allow you to include a header and footer (or not) on your page:

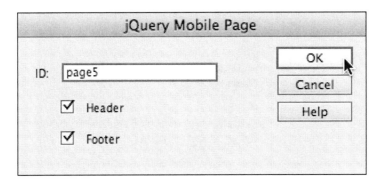

I wanted to show you the code before introducing this dialog box option so you'd have a better sense of what is happening, but having done that, I encourage you to use the dialog to save time.

Styling with theme swatches

The CSS file that is part of the jQuery Mobile library has five theme swatches. To get technical for a moment, all five of these swatches are built into a single CSS file. They are named a, b, c, d, and e. Each of these theme swatches provides a different, mobile-friendly (high contrast) color scheme for page backgrounds and font colors.

What this means is that, in a nutshell, you don't apply styling to jQuery Mobile pages by editing the CSS as you would for a normal web page. Instead, you change the HTML to apply one of the five theme swatches to any element on your page.

Isn't it a bit constricting to be limited to five theme swatches? Yes. But we'll solve that problem in *Chapter 9, Customizing Themes with ThemeRoller*, by creating our own custom theme swatches. First, let's get comfortable applying theme swatches.

Applying themes

What are "themes" in jQuery Mobile, exactly? The jQuery Mobile CSS file has built-in themes: a, b, c, d, and e. Again, these are not individual CSS stylesheet files; they are themes (sometimes referred to as swatches) within the CSS file. And each of these themes has a different color scheme.

You define which jQuery Mobile theme is applied to any element by using the `data-theme` property in HTML5. You can assign a theme swatch to any selected element with the **jQuery Mobile Swatches** panel.

View the panel by navigating to **Window | jQuery Mobile Swatches**. Click on any element in your page, and click on a swatch to assign that color scheme to the element. This works with Live view toggled to on, by the way.

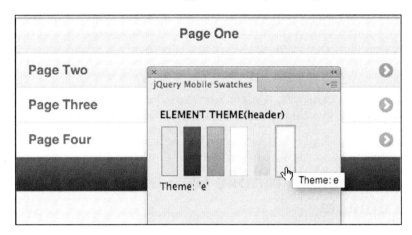

You can handcode theming. For example, to apply theme e to a page with a `div` ID of `page`, use this code:

```
<div data-role="page" id="page" data-theme="e">
```

Or to take a second example, if you wish to apply theme a to a content element on a page, use this code:

```
<div data-role="content" data-theme="a">
```

Editing CSS in jQuery Mobile pages

Because so much of the formatting in jQuery Mobile pages relies on the central CSS file that is part of the jQuery Mobile library, your options for defining custom CSS are quite limited. The CSS file that makes jQuery Mobile pages work is highly complex, with hundreds of CSS styles. Editing that stylesheet file can potentially undo the whole package and render your jQuery Mobile page dysfunctional.

If you are a high-level CSS coder, you can append your own CSS styles to the file provided as part of the jQuery Mobile package. But again, a high level of customization is available by using custom jQuery Mobile themes—something we'll explore in *Chapter 9, Customizing Themes with ThemeRoller*, of this book.

That said, if you do want to "go under the hood", here is a bit of advice on creating your own CSS styles for a jQuery Mobile page:

- You can identify and edit the `div` tag's styles—mostly `class` styles—to reformat content containers and other objects.

- You can identify and edit element (tag) rules in the CSS dialog. For example, you can redefine the heading and paragraph tags.

- In applying both of the preceding methods, you can draw on and apply the techniques explored in *Chapter 2, Using HTML5 for Page Structure*, except that you have to additionally take into account that many objects (`class` styles) in the jQuery Mobile page have specific rules for each of the five themes.

With these three bits of advice, readers who are experts at CSS coding might want to create their own CSS styles to enhance those provided as part of the jQuery Mobile pack.

Example – build a mobile web page with jQuery Mobile objects

To review and reinforce the concepts in this chapter, and to provide you with a quick set of steps to create your own jQuery Mobile page, let's walk through an example.

As with everything you do in Dreamweaver CS6, the prerequisite is that you are working on a defined Dreamweaver site. I'm calling mine `jqm`, but in any case if creating a site, if the essential nature of the process is not clear, review *Chapter 1, Creating Sites and Pages with Dreamweaver CS6*, and create the site.

1. Create a new jQuery Mobile page by navigating to **File | New**.

2. In the **New Document** dialog, choose **Page from Sample** in the **Category** column, **Mobile Starters** from the **Sample Folder** column, and **jQuery Mobile (CDN)** from the **Sample Page** column. Click on **Create**.

3. Save the page as `index.html`.

4. Set up a convenient workspace by choosing the **Split** view, setting the **Design** view **Window Size** to be `480` pixels wide and `800` pixels high, and viewing your **CSS Styles** panel.

5. Add a fifth page element to your jQuery Mobile site. To insert that page at the end of your site, click in the **Code** view to place your insertion point right before the closing `</body>` tag.

6. Insert the new page element by navigating to **Insert | jQuery Mobile | Page**. The **jQuery Mobile Page** dialog appears, with a preset prompt to add **page five**. Keep the checkbox options selected to include a header and footer on your page.

7. Even though Dreamweaver added a fifth page element, you still need to create a link to that element from your home page. Copy and paste the **Page Four** link on the home page of the jQuery Mobile site. Change the link text to **Page Five**, and change the link to **#page5** in the **Properties** inspector.

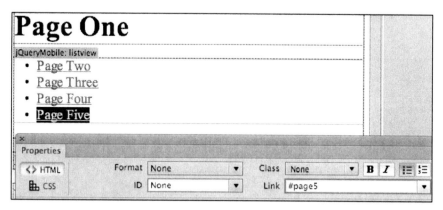

8. Customize the page content for each page. Need some inspiration for an example? Head over to Wikipedia's page for endangered species, and copy and paste some of the text (and pictures) into your various pages. When you copy and paste text from Wikipedia (or other sources), navigate to **Edit | Paste Special** to enable the **Paste Special** dialog and choose the **Text only** option to avoid copying links and styles as you paste the text into Dreamweaver.

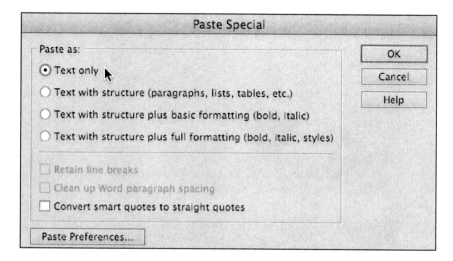

9. Check that the links on your home page element work. If you have set up pages for four endangered species, the home page should have links to each. And be sure to appropriately credit Wikipedia in your footer.

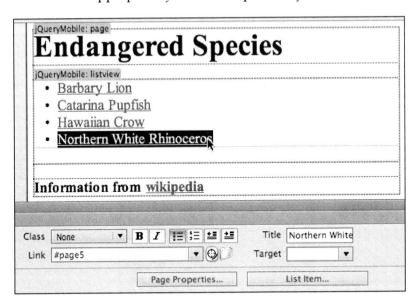

10. Test your site in Live view. Clicking each link on the home page element should open one of the four additional page elements.

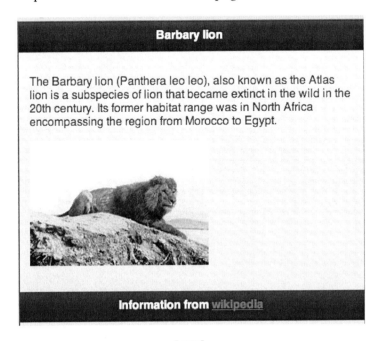

11. Make sure the **jQuery Mobile Swatches** panel is open (if not, navigate to **Window | jQuery Mobile Swatches**).

12. With Live View on, systematically work through your new site, selecting elements and applying swatch coloring to each element.

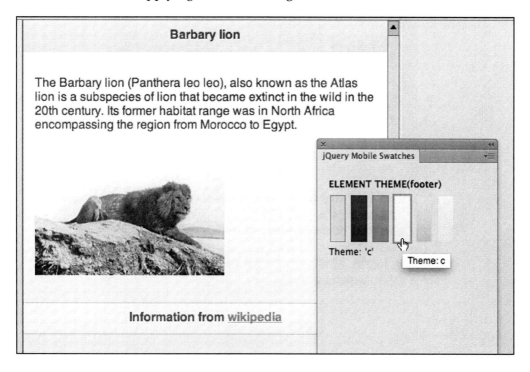

13. Save your page and navigate to **File | Preview in Browser**. Test your page in a browser. While testing in a browser in your development environment (a laptop or desktop computer) doesn't completely duplicate a mobile experience, it provides a good enough testing environment.

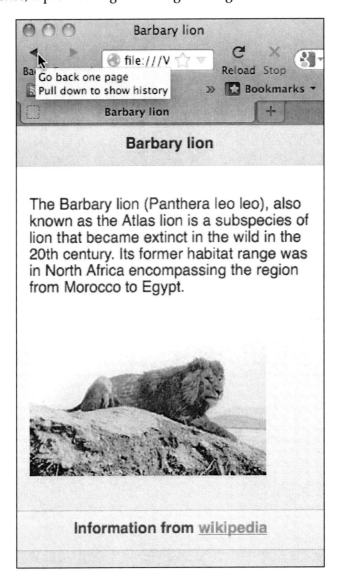

Summary

In this chapter, we covered the basic elements of creating complete jQuery Mobile pages in Dreamweaver CS6. These "pages" are pages on two levels. On one level, they are regular HTML pages using HTML5 (combined with CSS and JavaScript supplied via jQuery Mobile). On another level, this HTML page has jQuery data pages that are basically pages within a page. This technique allows us to create a mobile web page that allows visitors to navigate without having to wait for their mobile device to load additional pages.

For creating this jQuery Mobile page (with a set of data-pages), we relied on the Dreamweaver starter page. This page includes many of the most widely used jQuery Mobile elements. There are other useful jQuery Mobile page elements as well, and we'll explore them in the next chapter.

You edit the content of jQuery Mobile pages just as you would any HTML5 page. So all the blood, sweat, and tears you poured into mastering the basic techniques involved with customizing content of HTML5 pages in earlier chapters is paying off here. However, because page formatting and navigation rely so heavily on JavaScript (the jQuery Mobile library of scripts in particular), you need to rely more on Live View to see how pages will look compared to normal HTML5 pages.

Editing styles in jQuery Mobile are constrained to the fact that jQuery Mobile pages involve many CSS rules and jQuery Mobile CSS is organized into themes. In this chapter, you learned to apply theme swatches. In *Chapter 9, Customizing Themes with ThemeRoller*, we'll explore how to create custom themes.

In the basic jQuery Mobile page you've learned to create in this chapter, you have the foundation for creating very extensive jQuery Mobile sites. In the next chapter, we'll explore additional tools for creating more complex jQuery Mobile pages.

8

Enhancing Mobile Sites

In *Chapter 7, Creating Mobile Pages with jQuery Mobile*, we walked through the basic steps required to build a jQuery Mobile site in Dreamweaver. In the process, we focused on adding page-elements to a jQuery Mobile HTML page, and building listviews which links to those pages.

In doing that, we covered the bulk of what is required to build a functional jQuery Mobile site. You can browse the Web with a mobile device and find many professional-level sites that rely simply on jQuery Mobile page elements and listviews. In fact, it might be worthwhile to whip out your closest mobile device and browse a bit. You'll appreciate how essential basic listviews are to jQuery Mobile sites—similar to the one shown in the following screenshot for the San Francisco Chronicle:

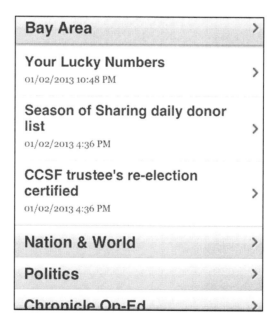

However, there's more to mobile page design than just listviews! There are alternate ways to provide page content in a mobile device. You can design pages with grids (columns). And you can employ expanding blocks that allow users to expand or contract vertically to present content.

If you do a bit more mobile browsing, you'll find sites that have some form of expandable/collapsible elements. For example, Google News uses expandable elements to show (or, by default, hide) **More sources** for news stories.

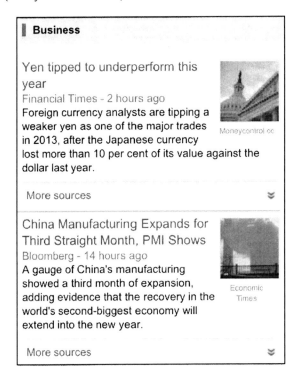

Moreover, there is the challenge of building really inviting and accessible forms for mobile devices that do not drive the users nuts by forcing them to attempt to click on a tiny checkbox or radio button with their fingernails, but instead provide nice, big form elements that are easy to tap in a smart phone.

We'll address and solve all these challenges in this chapter; the following are the topics covered in this chapter:

- Inserting layout grids
- Designing mobile pages with collapsible blocks
- Adding jQuery form objects
- Building a web-friendly site with collapsible blocks and a form

Inserting a layout grid

Columns play a diminished role in pages designed for mobile devices, compared to pages designed for full-sized viewports.

If you allowed lines of text to flow across the entire width of a 960-pixel page in a full-sized browser, the text would be hard to read. For that reason, and others, two or three column layouts are generally the best way to make content inviting and accessible in a full-sized browsing environment.

However, mobile viewports are different: there isn't much width in the viewport of a mobile phone, and even tablets have a narrower screen than laptops. Nevertheless, there are plenty of situations where it is useful to design page content in columns in mobile-friendly pages. When that is appropriate, the tool is jQuery grids. Grids allow you to easily build columns into jQuery Mobile page elements, as shown in the following menu:

Tables, div tags, and grids

For eons, or at least several years, tables were a staple of web design page layout technique. Creative designers adapted something that was intended to present rows and columns of data to lay out content on web pages.

We are past that era now. Instead, full-sized web pages are designed with `div` tags, something we explored in the first chapter, particularly in the *Using ID and class div styles for Layout* section. Tables are still around; older websites that were designed with tables are still online. Today, tables have been superseded by ID and class `div` tag styles because the latter is a much more powerful and flexible way to design pages.

But what about *using* tables for mobile page layout? Well, that technique is supported within jQuery Mobile. But we don't use tables for page layout in jQuery pages for the same reasons we don't use them in full-sized page design: tables are clunky, hard to apply global styles to, hard to update, and don't support a lot of the attributes that `div` containers support. That said, table design enthusiasts take note: you *can* design page layouts with tables in jQuery Mobile pages.

Can we use the good ol' `<div>` tags that served us so well in HTML to lay out page content in columns? Yes. But we have to do that in a special way that enables the formatting, animation, and interactivity that is so valuable in jQuery Mobile. I'll walk you through how that works in a moment.

The most flexible, standard way to design column layouts within a jQuery Mobile page is grids. The standard jQuery Mobile CSS file comes with a set of defined class styles called `ui-block` and `ui-grid`. Moreover, there are two sets of these styles, one for two-column layouts, and one for three-column layouts.

Dreamweaver's jQuery Mobile widget for a layout grid does a very complete job of generating a wide variety of grids, with definable numbers of columns and rows. Remember, as you generate such grids, that you are designing for a relatively narrow viewport of one kind or another, and will want to be restrained in how many columns (and rows) you generate.

But as you are vigilant from a design standpoint, you can relax on the technical front. The Layout Grid widget in Dreamweaver strings together fairly complex combinations of the 2-column and 3-column grids to create grids of four, five, six, and more columns if you choose to do that.

Generating grids in Dreamweaver

To generate a layout grid in a jQuery Mobile page, make sure your insertion point is in the `content` div data-role. An easy way to do that is to select the text content in the code that is generated when you create a jQuery Mobile "page", and replace it with the layout grid, or, to place your cursor after the "content" placeholder text.

Then, navigate to **Insert | jQuery Mobile | Layout Grid**. The **jQuery Mobile Layout Grid** dialog opens. Select a value for **Rows** and **Columns**, and click on **OK** to generate the layout grid, as shown in the following screenshot:

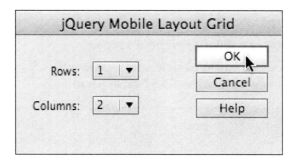

Defining styles for layout grids

The jQuery Mobile layout grid uses two class styles—`.ui-grid-a` for two-column grids, and `.ui-grid-b` for three-column grids. Dreamweaver, as noted, will generate HTML from the **jQuery Mobile Layout Grid** dialog to string together combinations of these two grids to create grids of more than three columns. In addition, Dreamweaver generates `.ui-grid` class styles to define specific block formatting.

The point? By editing the properties of `.ui-grid` and `.ui-block` class styles, you can define the appearance of elements of layout grids.

As you do that, avoid editing the widths of the grids or blocks, or the margins, padding or border dimensions. Changing those properties will destroy the generated layout. But you can edit background colors and images.

Let's walk through how this works.

The `.ui-grid-a` class style (that defines a two-column grid) can be overridden by a local grid class style. But that doesn't open up much formatting freedom since the grid itself only provides the frame that holds the two blocks.

To edit the look of the left block (`.ui-block-a`), follow the ensuing steps:

1. Click on the **New CSS Styles Rule** icon at the bottom of the **CSS Styles** panel. The **New CSS Rule** dialog box opens.

2. In the **Selector Type** field, select **Class**.

3. In the **Selector Name** field, enter `.ui-block-a`.

4. In the **Rule Definition** box, select **This Document Only**.

5. Click **OK** to close the dialog and open the **CSS Rule Definition** dialog for `.ui-block-a`.

6. In the **background-color** field, select a background color.

7. In the box category, enter a height of `200px`.

8. Click **OK** to define this local style, and examine the effect in **Live** view, and examine the style rules in the **CSS Styles** panel.

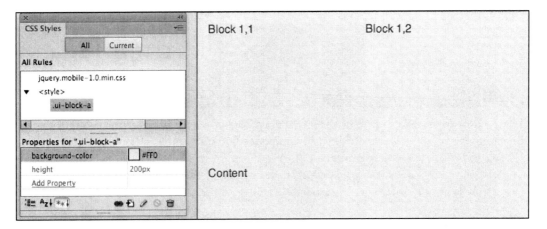

Let's reflect on what happened and why. Many of the attributes of the `.ui-block-a` class style, that defines how left-side blocks within a grid appear, are fixed as part of the universal CSS style file that makes jQuery Mobile tick. We linked to that CSS file when we generated a new jQuery Mobile page in Dreamweaver.

But some of the attributes of a `.ui-block-a` class style are not fixed, and we can edit them in a local stylesheet that applies only to our HTML page. `background-color` and `height` are two attributes we can edit, and provide a way to customize the look of our grid.

And, of course, we can apply the same technique to the `.ui-block-b` class style that defines how right-side blocks within a grid appear, as illustrated in the following screenshot:

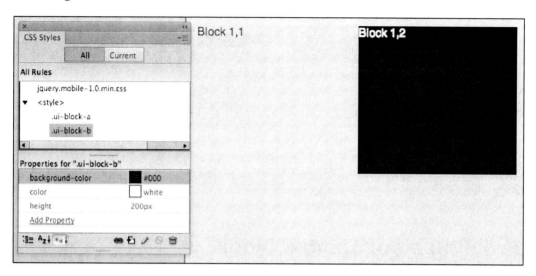

How useful are formatted grids and blocks? They are increasingly useful because more and more mobile designers are using jQuery Mobile to create multicolumn layouts for larger and medium-sized tablets. Blocks and grids provide the most flexible, accessible tool for column layout in jQuery Mobile.

Designing Mobile Pages with collapsible blocks

jQuery Mobile Pages, as you saw in the previous chapter (*Chapter 7, Creating Mobile Pages with jQuery Mobile*), essentially create the sense of navigating from page to page while relying on JavaScript to actually display and hide content. That is the technique used in the sample jQuery Mobile pages generated in Dreamweaver.

Expandable blocks operate on a similar principle—they show and hide content depending on a visitor's actions. However, with expandable panels, this takes place through sections of the page appearing to expand or shrink, as shown in the following screenshot:

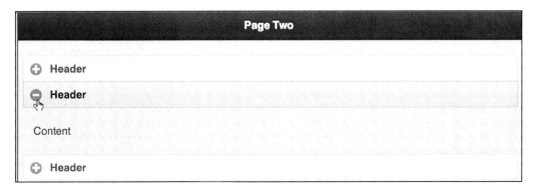

Building a collapsible block

Like other jQuery Mobile objects, collapsible panels require the framework of a jQuery Mobile page. So, the first step in implementing them is to create a jQuery Mobile page. This is done by navigating to **Insert** | **jQuery Mobile** | **Page**. We explored the options for generating jQuery Mobile pages in Dreamweaver a bit earlier in this chapter.

Once you have generated a jQuery Mobile page, with all the attendant CSS and JavaScript files that make that work, you can define collapsible panels. Do that by setting your insertion point (this is most easily done in the code side of **Split** view, with **Live** view turned on).

Navigate to **Insert** | **jQuery Mobile** | **Collapsible Block**. No dialog appears, Dreamweaver generates HTML code for a set of three collapsible sections within the block.

After our experience with starter pages in the previous chapter, and layout grids in this chapter, and with your background in HTML5 and CSS, you've already conceptualized how we will customize the look and content of the collapsible block. We can change the formatting through a combination of using the jQuery Mobile data-theme sets and customized CSS styles. Moreover, we can change the content by editing the HTML, including by copying and pasting collapsible blocks.

Changing the initial block state

The entire set of collapsible elements is defined by the following code:

```
<div data-role="collapsible-set">
```

In between the opening and closing `<div>` tags for a collapsible set are individual expandable blocks:

```
<div data-role="collapsible" data-collapsed="true"> </div>
```

Or blocks that are expanded by default when the page opens, defined with this code:

```
<div data-role="collapsible">
```

By default, the first of the three expandable sections is expanded when the page opens, and the other two are collapsed. Adding the `data-collapsed="true"` parameter to the initially opened panel changes it to collapsed when the page opens.

```
<div data-role="content">
   <div data-role="collapsible-set">
     <div data-role="collapsible">
       <h3>Header</h3>
       <p>Content</p>
     </div>
     <div data-role="collapsible" data-collapsed="true">
       <h3>Header</h3>
       <p>Content</p>
     </div>
     <div data-role="collapsible" data-collapsed="true">
       <h3>Header</h3>
       <p>Content</p>
     </div>
```

Moreover, conversely removing `data-collapsed="true"` from a panel changes it to display expanded when the page opens.

Changing block data-themes and styles

We can add a `data-theme` parameter to any data block. For example, changing `<div data-role="collapsible">` to `<div data-role="collapsible" data-theme="e">` applies data-theme e (a yellow and red color scheme) to that block, as shown in the following screenshot:

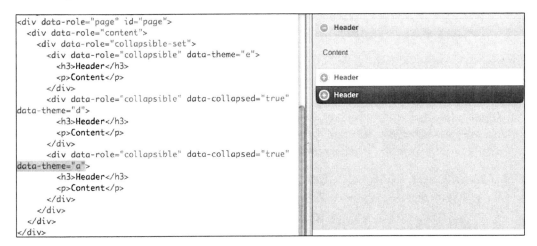

Obviously, there are rather severe limits to what you can do with the default set of theme color schemes. Not to worry, in the next chapter, we'll explore customizing themes.

CSS styles associated with the collapsible panels can be customized in the **CSS Styles** panel. These styles generally start with `.ul-collapsible`.

The `.ui-collapsible-contain` style, for example, controls many of the properties of the content of an expanded block, as shown in the following screenshot:

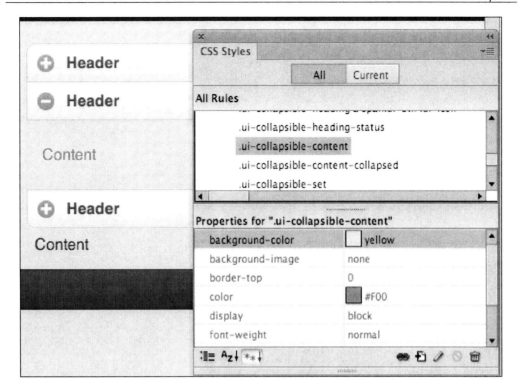

Be cautious in changing dimensions of the `.ul-collapsible` class styles. Avoid changing padding, margins, and borders, as messing with these parameters might wreck the collapsible columns. You can customize fonts, colors, font sizes, background colors, and other properties. And, again, we'll explore a whole world of themes customization in the next chapter.

Editing collapsible block HTML

Depending on your inclinations, you can edit the content of collapsible blocks either in Design view, with Live view turned off, or in Live view, by editing the content on the Code side of Split view. In either case, you just add HTML tags (such as headings, paragraph tags, ordered or unordered lists, and so on), and text, images, and media.

If you edit content in the **Code** side of **Split** view, click on the **Refresh** button in the **Document** toolbar periodically to update the **Design** side of the view.

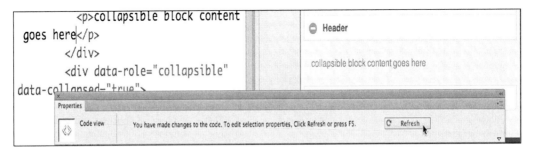

At this stage of the game, you've figured out on your own how to add a collapsible block to a set: just copy, paste, and edit an existing block.

Since you asked (I read your mind), yes, you can embed collapsible blocks within a collapsible block. But the point, remember, is to keep mobile page layouts fairly simple, so, as the saying goes, when organizing content for mobile, less is more.

Adding jQuery form objects

The experience of filling out a form in a mobile device environment is substantially different than filling out a form on a laptop or desktop. There is no mouse, or even (often) a *Tab* key to navigate between form fields. Big fingers and tiny options in pop-up menus make for a bad match.

A form that might work fine in a full-sized browser may well be terribly uninviting and inconvenient in a mobile device. Take Apple's store locator (shown in the following screenshot) for example, it is poorly designed for mobile users, requiring mobile users to invoke their frustrating keyboards to enter a zip code into a tiny text field:

Part of the solution to that challenge is that mobile devices often convert form fields to more accessible elements. For example, options in a select menu might display much larger when tapped, making it easier to make a selection. The same Apple form I just criticized has a better option for choosing a product—a drop-down menu that is easier to access with a mobile device and chubby fingers like mine.

The other part of the solution to making forms accessible and inviting in mobile devices is to implement new form fields, such as sliders (where visitors can select from a range of values by sliding a thumb on a bar) or flip toggle switches (with easy to use "on" and "off" switch options) to make filling out forms online more functional and more fun.

The following form utilizes both a flip toggle (**On** switch and a value slider (0-100)):

Forms in Dreamweaver

Dreamweaver has historically provided three methods for creating forms. You can, of course, define forms and form fields using HTML in Code view. You can generate forms by navigating to **Insert | Form** and define a form, then within it insert form fields (such as a text field) and the requisite buttons (such as a **Submit** button to make the form do something).

More recent versions of Dreamweaver, including Dreamweaver CS6, have added Spry Validation form fields that first test data (for example, to see if it looks like an e-mail address) before allowing a visitor to submit the form. I note this history because a) you can't get where you're going if you don't know where you've been, or whatever that saying is; and b) all these techniques still work in mobile devices, so if you know any or all of them, you can supplement the new jQuery Mobile form tools in Dreamweaver with those tools.

Here, however, we'll focus on the jQuery Mobile form tools that are geared to creating mobile-friendly forms, and include form fields such as the slider, and the toggle switch, that until now have not been easily accessible in Dreamweaver.

Before diving into those tools, here's the world's most compressed course in creating forms in Dreamweaver (in general, not just using jQuery Mobile form tools):

1. All form fields (such as a text field, or a **Submit** button) have to be enclosed within a single set of `<form>` tags.

2. In order to work, forms must have a defined action. For forms that connect to server-side scripts (scripts written in programming languages such as PHP or Perl, and reside on a server), the action is a link to post the data to the location of that script at a server. There are many free, fairly intuitive online resources for generating such scripts, with directions on how to upload them to your server and connect them to a form. One such resource is `TheSiteWizard.com`. A very simple, but functional action is to simply e-mail form content to an e-mail address using the action `mailto:xxx@xxx.xxx`, where `xxx@xxx.xxx` is an e-mail address. This simple solution then launches an e-mail client (program) and prompts the user to e-mail the form content to the provided e-mail address.

With those two basic rules in mind, let's examine tools in Dreamweaver for creating forms with particularly mobile-friendly form fields.

Creating a jQuery Mobile form

Like the other jQuery Mobile objects we've examined in this chapter, jQuery Mobile form elements can only be inserted into an already generated jQuery Mobile page. But beyond that, it is also necessary to create both a form and a **Submit** button using more traditional form features in Dreamweaver. So, the process of setting up a form that will enclose jQuery Mobile form elements is as follows:

1. Create a jQuery Mobile page.
2. Insert a form inside that jQuery Mobile page with a **Submit** (button).
3. Then you can add specifically mobile-friend jQuery Mobile form fields to that form.

That three-step process isn't the only way to create jQuery Mobile forms, and it doesn't incorporate every possible option for such forms. But it is a basic foundation for making it possible to implement jQuery Mobile form elements.

Let's work through an example, creating a basic form that, when submitted, will send content to an e-mail address through an e-mail client. These steps assume, of course, that you are working in a defined Dreamweaver site, and that you have created an HTML5 page with a jQuery Mobile page. With those pieces in place, the following steps flesh out the "three-step process" outlined in rougher strokes previously:

1. Inside the jQuery Mobile page (you can select the placeholder "content" text in either the **Code** view or **Design** view to make sure you're doing this right), navigate to **Insert | Form | Form**. The **Tag Editor – form** dialog appears. Only the options in the **General** tab are essential for creating a form.

2. In the **Action** field, enter `mailto:[an email address]` using, of course, a real e-mail address. If you were working with a form linked to a server-side script, you would enter the URL of that script here.

3. Select **post** from the **Method** pop-up, this is the method almost always used to send form data to a location.

4. The **Encoding type** parameters are defined by the script that is managing the data. If you are uploading via e-mail, enter `text/plain`.

5. Enter a name for your form in the **Name** box.

6. The **Target** pop-up allows you to select `_blank` if you want to open the linked form script in a new browser window (generally this is not necessary).

7. After completing the **Tag Editor – form** dialog, click **OK** to generate the form.

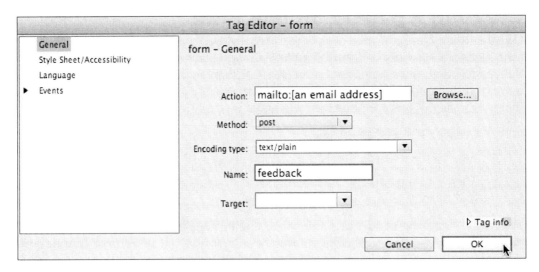

This set of steps simply defines a form. There are no form fields in that form yet, so nothing in **Live** view indicates there even is a form. You can see the form code in **Code** view of course, and you can see the form itself, indicated by a red outline, in the **Design** view with **Live** view turned off.

Remember rule #1 from earlier in this section: in order to be acted on by a form action, *all form fields have to be inside a form*. So make sure you are clear on where your form is on your page, even though it has no content as yet.

With your cursor *inside your form*, navigate to **Insert | Form | Button**. We are not (quite) yet at the stage of integrating special jQuery Mobile form fields, so this option will be available by simply navigating to **Insert | Form**. When the **Input Form Accessibility Attributes** dialog appears, you do not need to enter anything in any of the fields, simply click on **OK** to generate a **Submit** button.

We now have the basic elements of a form: the form itself with a defined action, and a **Submit** button. Next, it is time to add the jQuery Mobile form fields.

Special mobile form fields

As noted earlier, mobile devices often have built-in interface tools to make form content more accessible. So does jQuery Mobile. When you place standard HTML form fields, such as textboxes, checkboxes, and buttons, jQuery Mobile substitutes custom form fields that are more accessible in mobile devices. Checkboxes are made larger, select menus pop up lists of large buttons, form field labels and field names are resized to maximize screen real-estate.

So, some of the "special" form fields available from the jQuery Mobile submenu are simply adaptations of standard HTML form fields. Others are new to the HTML form field set. In either case, the jQuery Mobile form fields include, as noted, special formatting that makes them more mobile-friendly.

Let's examine three of these form fields, and based on those examples, you'll be able to work with additional form fields in the jQuery Mobile set. In each of these examples, *be sure that you are inserting the jQuery Mobile form fields within the set of* <form> *tags*.

Inserting a text input field

Text fields are the most flexible way of collecting data in forms. They are used to collect usernames, passwords, e-mail addresses, shipping addresses, and more.

To insert a jQuery Mobile text input field in a form, navigate to **Insert | jQuery Mobile | Text Input** (if you want to allow multiple-line input, select **Text Area** instead). The jQuery Mobile text input field is automatically sized, but you have to replace the label placeholder text (**Text Input**) with your own text. You can do this in Design view (with Live View off) or in Split view.

You can also replace the input name by changing the default field name for the text field by editing the code `name="textinput"` with another field name inside the quotes. But avoid spaces and special characters (stick to letters and numbers). So, for example, to rename a text input field named `email`, you would change this code to `name="email"`.

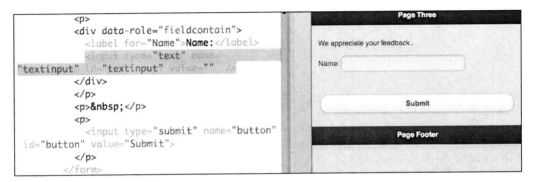

Inserting a slider

Everybody's rating everything these days. You might not have read much physics, but how would you rate Bosonic string theory on a scale of 1-100? Well, ok… there *are* valid reasons to include rating options in a mobile form. And, if you're going to include a "rate this … (whatever)" in your form, you should make it easy for people to do that.

Enter the *slider*, a particularly handy way to input values in a mobile form.

To insert a slider in a jQuery Mobile form, navigate to **Insert | jQuery Mobile | Slider**. Customize the slider as follows:

1. Replace the **Slider** label text with your own text.

2. Replace the `value="0"` code with a value that will display by default.

3. Replace the `min="0"` code with any value you select that will be the minimum value.

4. Replace the `max="0"` code with any value you select that will be the maximum value.

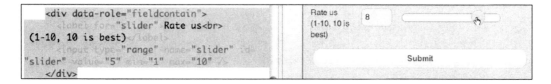

Inserting a toggle switch

Toggle switches provide a handy way for large fingers to easily select "yes" or "no"; "in" or "out"; or make some other two-option choice in a mobile device.

To insert a toggle switch in a jQuery Mobile form, navigate to **Insert | jQuery Mobile | Flip Toggle Switch**.

Customize the toggle switch as follows:

1. Replace the **Option** label text with your own text.

2. Replace `Off` (not in quotes) in the code `<option value="off">Off</option>` with your own text.

3. Replace `On` (not in quotes) in the code `<option value="on">On</option>` with your own text.

Building a page with collapsible blocks and a mobile-friendly form

Let's walk through a specific example to summarize, review, flesh out, and provide a model of building jQuery Mobile collapsible blocks in Dreamweaver, and mix in a mobile-friendly form.

Surveys tell us that a huge percentage of people looking to grab a taco somewhere search online for a place to get one—on their mobile devices. So let's use my non-existent taco stand at Coney Island as a model for this recipe, and you can easily adapt it to your own needs.

The mobile page we build will have four collapsible blocks: menu, location, place orders, and a bit about the taco shop. In the course of building it, we'll walk through creating four collapsible blocks, and embedding a form within one of the blocks. Here we go:

1. Of course, we're assuming you are working within a Dreamweaver site. If not, create a new one or open an existing one. Then navigate to **File | New** and in the **New Document** dialog, select **Blank Page** in the **Category** column, **HTML** in the **Page Type** column, **<none>** in the **Layout** column, and **HTML5** from the **DocType** popup. Then click on **Create**.

2. Navigate to **File | Save**, and save the file as `index.html`. As this is going to be a one-page site, the `index.html` filename will open the page when the site's URL is addressed in a browser. Assign a page title of "Mobile Tacos".

3. At this stage of the process, by default, your cursor is in between the set of `<body>` tags. That's right where it should be. Insert a jQuery Mobile page by navigating to **Insert | jQuery Mobile | Page**. As we are going to be keeping this project relatively simple and standard (but not *too* simple, or standard—don't worry), you can select the **Remote (CDN)** link type option, and we'll avail ourselves of the online version of the jQuery Mobile CSS file. With **Remote (CDN)** selected, click on **OK**.

4. The **jQuery Mobile Page** dialog opens. Click on **OK** with the default settings.

5. Replace the original `Header` placeholder text with "Coney Island Tacos". Or, you can depart from my recipe right from the start, and freelance your own content from here on. Replace the footer text with the imaginary website of Coney Island Tacos – `www.coneyislandtacos.com`. Navigate to **Insert | Hyperlink** if you wish to define the hyperlink.

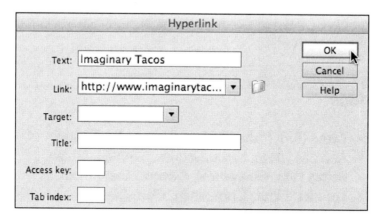

6. Define a work environment: select **Split View** and then **480x800** from the **Window Size** popup at the bottom of the **Design** view. Turn on **Live View**.

7. Start with applying one of the jQuery Mobile themes for formatting. In the code side of **Split** view, enter the code `data-theme="e"` or experiment with other themes (try `a`, `b`, `c`, `d`, or `e`).

```
<div id="page" data-role="page" data-theme="e">
```

Now let's walk through the process of adding four collapsible panels to our site:

1. Select the placeholder `content` text, and navigate to **Insert | jQuery Mobile | Collapsible Block**. Copy and paste one of the sets of collapsible block code to create a forth block. The code is:

```
<div data-role="collapsible" data-collapsed="true">

    <h3>Header</h3>
  <p>Content</p>
</div>
```

2. Customize the headers for all four blocks. You'll find the headers enclosed in `<h3>` codes. I'm going with: **Menu, Email Order, Find / Call Us**, and **About Coney Island Tacos** as headers, but feel free to improvise.

3. Customize the content of all the collapsible blocks *except* the **Email Order** block — we'll create a form for that next.

4. In the **Email Order** block (or whichever block you are using in a custom project for an input form), select the placeholder content text and navigate to **Insert | Form | Form**. In the **Tag Editor – form** dialog, make the action mailto:youremail@youremail.xxx (substituting your own e-mail address). Change the method to **POST**. Enter text/plain in the **Encoding Type** field and click on **OK**. Here, it might be helpful to pop out of live view to create the input form. Enter Order Form inside the form and press *Return* or *Enter* to create a new line.

jQueryMobile: collapsible-set

Menu

- Tacos ($3): Fish, Chicken, Veggie, Beef, Pork
- Add ons (free): Salsa, Lettuce, Tomato, Onion
- Extras ($2): Guacamole, Cheese, Extra meat
- Tortillas: Flour, Corn (soft), Corn (hard)

5. Making sure your insertion point is inside the form, navigate to **Insert | jQuery Mobile | Select Menu**. Change the label to **Taco**. Click on the **Select** menu itself, and use the **List Values** button in the **Properties** inspector to open the **List Values** dialog. Enter labels (which appear in the form) and values (which are sent via e-mail when the form is submitted), using the **+** button to add new rows, and the up and down arrows to reorder items as necessary.

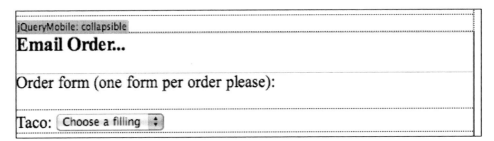

jQueryMobile: collapsible

Email Order...

Order form (one form per order please):

Taco: [Choose a filling ⬍]

6. Add additional select menu to allow people to select a taco shell.

7. Still within the form, navigate to **Insert | jQuery Mobile | Checkbox**. In the **jQuery Mobile Checkbox** dialog, enter Sides in the **Name** box, and select four checkboxes and a horizontal layout, and click on **OK**. Edit the labels right in **Design** view in the **Document** window, and use the **Properties** inspector to define values for each checkbox that match the labels.

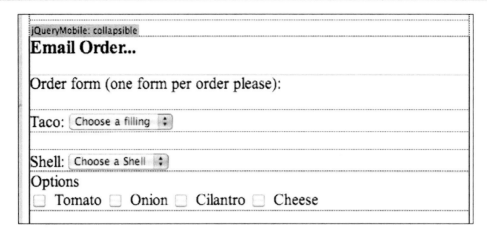

8. Complete the form by inserting a **Submit** button. Again, *make sure your insertion point is inside the form*, and navigate to **Insert | Form | Button**. Click on **OK** without making any selection as a **Submit** button is the default.

9. To customize the look of the page, create a new class style. Use the **New CSS Rule** option at the bottom of the **CSS Styles** panel to create a new CSS rule. Name the class style Format. As we are using a remote version of the associated CSS file, and as this is a one-page site, we can break the rule of relying exclusively on linked, external stylesheets, so select **(This Document Only)** from the pop-up menu at the bottom of the **New CSS Rule** dialog, and click on **OK**.

10. Define some custom properties, such as font family, font size, and font color. Use the **Properties** inspector, as shown in the following screenshot, to apply the class style to selected elements on your page:

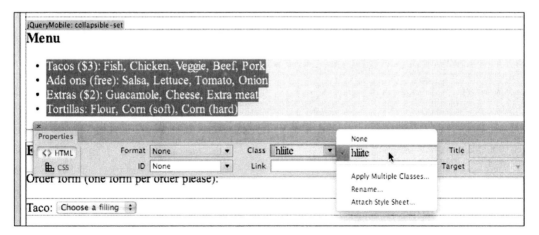

11. You can further customize the project by creating additional class styles and applying them.

12. You can test the order form in a browser.

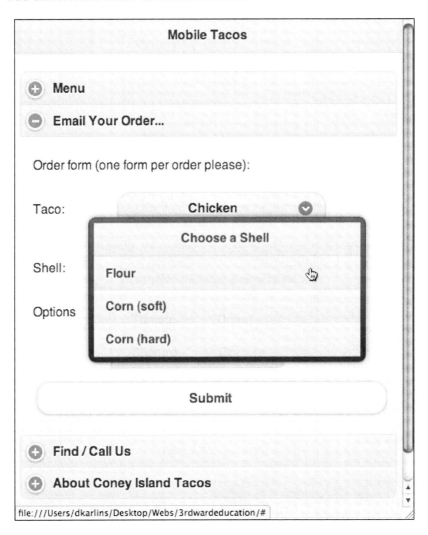

Summary

One page-design technique in jQuery Mobile is a layout grid. A layout grid, with blocks, is essentially `div` style columns, but with special properties that make the columns display effectively in mobile devices.

The two most important jQuery Mobile techniques we introduced in this chapter are collapsible blocks, and jQuery Mobile form objects. Collapsible blocks expand and collapse, and provide a very comfortable way to present content in a small viewport. Adding jQuery form objects creates more mobile-friendly versions of familiar input form objects (such as text boxes), but also enables new form fields such as sliders and toggle flip switches.

To customize the look and feel of jQuery Mobile-based pages, we can utilize the broad brush formatting of data-themes, supplemented with custom CSS. But to really uncork the power of themes, we need to create our own custom theme color swatches. We'll do that in the next chapter.

9
Customizing Themes with ThemeRoller

At this stage of our journey, we've explored the structuring of basic and more complex jQuery Mobile pages with Dreamweaver CS6. What's missing? Style! We haven't yet customized fonts, font colors, backgrounds, and all the other things that we learned to do with CSS stylesheets in the early chapters of this book.

But normal CSS styling rules apply only in a very limited sense when we are styling jQuery Mobile pages. Why? Because jQuery Mobile pages rely on a centralized, and rather massive CSS stylesheet file. The file includes five sets of color scheme swatches. In this chapter, you'll learn to apply those color swatches in Dreamweaver CS6.

But five sets of color scheme swatches are not many. In order to seriously customize how jQuery Mobile pages look, it is necessary to alter the theme, which is another way of saying you have to customize the centrally distributed CSS stylesheet. In the latter half of this chapter, we'll walk through how to create customized CSS files, themes, using **ThemeRoller**, an online utility embraced by Adobe.

The following topics will be covered:

- Understanding formatting with jQuery Mobile themes in Dreamweaver
- Applying jQuery Mobile themes to page elements
- Applying jQuery Mobile themes to specific elements within pages
- Customizing jQuery Mobile themes with ThemeRoller

Applying jQuery Mobile theme swatches

There are five standard jQuery Mobile data-themes (or themes, for short). They are: a, b, c, d, and, as you might have guessed, e. The five standard themes are built into the large centralized CSS stylesheet file to which we link all jQuery Mobile pages.

 If you examine that CSS file, you'll see that most of the CSS styles in that stylesheet have an -a, -b, -c, -d, or -e in the style name.

Again, the basic concept here is that the five theme swatches (a, b, c, d, and e) are all stored in the single CSS stylesheet file that every jQuery Mobile page links to. That link is built into jQuery Mobile pages generated in Dreamweaver.

Examining the five data-themes

It is not possible in a printed book, or even our e-book edition, to provide a dynamic, animated, interactive demonstration of the five default jQuery Mobile theme swatches. The best way to see how they work is to do either of the following:

- Apply them to a page in Dreamweaver
- Look them up at the jQuery Mobile site where you can interact with and compare all five themes as shown in the following screenshot:

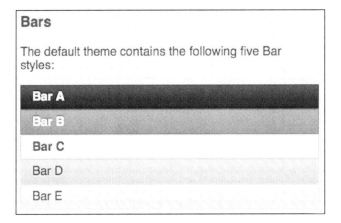

 The URL for the jQuery Mobile page that demonstrates these theme swatches changes periodically. But you can find it at www. jquerymobile.com. There will be a link to the Theme Framework section of the site that is easily accessible from the site's home page.

As a quick text reference, here are simplified descriptions of each of the themes:

- Theme *a* is a high-contrast, dark gray-based color scheme that is accessible in all kinds of lighting situations.

- Theme *b* is a white-type-on-blue-background style that's a bit less accessible, but inviting and still high-contrast.

- Theme *c* is kind of the inverse of theme *a*. Instead of white type on a dark gray background, it presents dark gray type on a light gray background.

- Theme *d* is hardly distinguishable from theme *c* but is higher contrast with a white instead of a light-gray background behind dark gray type.

- Theme *e* has a yellow-to-orange gradient background that is inviting and more upbeat than other themes.

To apply a theme swatch in Dreamweaver CS6, follow the given steps:

1. With your Dreamweaver site defined, navigate to **File** | **New** to open the **New Document** dialog.

2. Choose **Sample** | **Page** from the **Category** column on the left, **Mobile Starters** from the **Sample Folder** column, and **jQuery Mobile (CDN)** from the **Sample Page** column and click on **Create** to generate a new page.

3. With the jQuery Mobile page open, use the **Split** view, and turn the **Live** view on.

4. Save the page. We'll use Dreamweaver CS6's **jQuery Mobile Swatches** panel in a moment, and that panel requires that you save a page first. With the page saved, navigate to **Window** | **jQuery Mobile Swatches** to display the **jQuery Mobile Swatches** panel.

5. Click on any of the five available theme swatches (the swatch on the far left assigns no theme), as shown in the following screenshot:

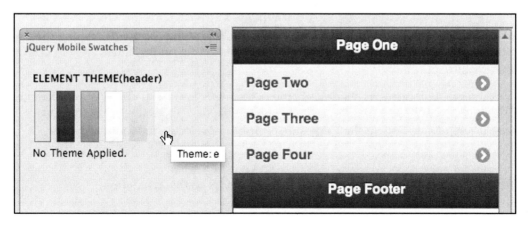

You can also assign a data-theme to any element in the **Code** view. Apply jQuery Mobile themes with the following syntax:

```
data-theme="x"
```

Where "x" is a, b, c, d, or e. Here's an example applying data-theme e to the first page element:

```
(<div data-role="page" id="page" data-theme="e">
```

That data-theme code can be applied within any jQuery Mobile element. After you edit a data-theme in the **Code** view, click on the **Refresh** button in the **Document** toolbar to refresh the view, as shown in the following screenshot:

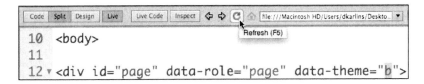

 Users of versions of Dreamweaver prior to CS6 will not have access to the **jQuery Mobile Swatches** panel, and will have to apply data-themes in code view, as discussed previously.

Applying themes to specific elements

When you apply a data-theme to an entire page element, you define a color scheme for that page element. But you can also apply data-themes to any element within data-pages to tweak exactly how each element appears.

But here's a challenge; you can only see how a data-theme looks when you have the **Live** view turned on in Dreamweaver. However, with **Live** view turned on, it is difficult to select elements to apply a theme too, because often when you click on an element (such as a link in a **List** view), the link works, and you no longer see it in the preview window. So, I generally suggest relying on the **Code** view to apply data-themes.

For example, you can assign a data-theme to the main listview that was generated by default with our jQuery Mobile sample page (on the first page element of the jQuery Mobile site). To do that, in the **Code** side of **Split** view, locate the following code:

```
<ul data-role="listview">
```

To apply a data-theme b, we can add this parameter to the listview:

```
<ul data-role="listview" data-theme="b">
```

Save your page and examine the effect in the **Live** view.

You can apply data-themes to *any* element. That includes elements *within* a `listview`. For example, we can assign a different data-theme to each list item in the `listview`. To do that, add data-theme definitions to the three `<li>` tags in the first page element. The following code applies data-themes `c`, `d`, and `e` respectively to the list elements:

```
<li data-theme="c"><a href="#page2" >Page Two</a></li>
<li data-theme="d"><a href="#page3" >Page Three</a></li>
<li data-theme="e"><a href="#page4" >Page Four</a></li>
```

Customizing themes with ThemeRoller

The mobile world would be a rather dull, conformist place if every site was constrained by the color options available from the five default themes available in the jQuery Mobile CSS file.

The most accessible, powerful tool for creating custom themes is ThemeRoller. ThemeRoller is an online application that rolls together a set of swatches into a theme. ThemeRoller creates as many as 26 separate swatches.

Themes and swatches

The five jQuery Mobile theme swatches (a, b, c, d, and e) are often referred to, for shorthand, as themes. But technically speaking, these sets of colors and graphical elements are swatches within a theme. A jQuery Mobile theme is actually a set of swatches within the CSS stylesheet associated with the jQuery Mobile package.

The aesthetics of mobile color schemes

Before setting you loose to create custom themes in ThemeRoller, let me review a few basic rules for designing effective, inviting, accessible color schemes for mobile devices.

- All web design color schemes are built around a set of five colors. Those five colors can be any set of colors you choose. But the reason constraining that set to five is that fewer would be boring, and more than five colors would create a visual clutter—too much color without coherence or purpose.

- Neutral colors, such as white, black, shades of gray, and blue, don't count as part of a set of five. Use as much of them as necessary.

- Mobile sites require high contrast color schemes. Slate gray text on a charcoal screen might be an effective color scheme for users on powerfully backlit laptops in environments with fine-tunable lighting. But in the bright Sun, that color scheme will look like a solid block of black.

- Using gradient blends that flow one color into another, make mobile sites inviting.

In professional mobile design workflow, a designer picks a color scheme and provides you with color values for the set of five colors to use.

Launching ThemeRoller

You can launch ThemeRoller by clicking on the **Get More Themes** link at the bottom of the **jQuery Mobile Swatches** panel, as shown in the following screenshot:

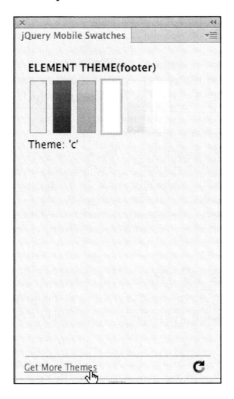

Alternately (or if you are using an older version of Dreamweaver), you can just navigate in your browser to the jQuery Mobile's page for ThemeRoller at http://jquerymobile.com/themeroller/.

ThemeRoller is an online, open-source project that has been embraced by, but is not part of, Adobe Dreamweaver. As such, ThemeRoller is not as stable and easy to reliably document as a traditional software application such as Dreamweaver. This means that what I write about ThemeRoller here is going to be generally accurate when you read this book, but you should expect a few discrepancies as ThemeRoller evolves. I'll prepare you for those. That said, ThemeRoller is a very powerful tool. It allows us to fully customize the look and feel of jQuery Mobile sites. It's relatively easy to use, and adds substantial value to what we as developers can add to a website.

As emphasized in the preceding tip, ThemeRoller is an evolving online resource, so your screen will look somewhat different from, but pretty much like the following screenshot. If a **Get Rolling** button is visible, as in the following screenshot, click on that button to make the informational box go away, and begin working in ThemeRoller.

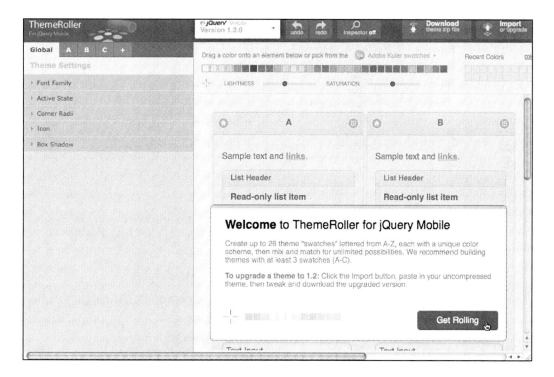

Defining global theme attributes

There are two sections to define a theme in ThemeRoller: **global**, and **swatch**. Global attributes include properties such as font, that apply to *all* swatches. Color schemes are defined by swatch.

You navigate between global elements and individual swatches using tabs at the top-left corner of the **ThemeRoller** window, as shown in the following screenshot:

Normally, it makes sense to start by defining global theme attributes for a custom theme.

Global theme settings include the following:

- **Font Family**: This lets you choose a set of fonts, starting with your preferred display font, just as you would if you were defining a CSS font-family property for the `<body>` tag in a normal web page
- **Active State**: This set of options control active links display
- **Corner Radii**: This setting defines the size of the radius on the corners of the rounded-corner boxes
- **Icon**: This option defines the color and style of icons
- **Box Shadow**: These settings control color, opacity, and the size of any drop-shadows applied to boxes

All these properties are defined for your entire jQuery Mobile page—that is all the elements (including page elements) in your site. And they have to be global. Why? Think about the corner radius on a `listview`, for example. If that corner radius is different in different color swatches, your `listview` would vary in shape depending on what color you assigned to it.

To edit global theme attributes in the **Global** tab on the left-hand side of the ThemeRoller app window, click on the expand triangle associated with that attribute to see available choices.

Some global theme settings are very important, others more obscure. **Font Family**, **Corner Radii**, and **Box Shadow** are the three attributes that have the most substantial impact on your custom theme.

To change the defined font family, enter new fonts (separated by commas) in the **FONT** field in the **Font Family** tab. When you click outside the field, the edited font family displays on the right-hand side preview window, as shown in the following screenshot:

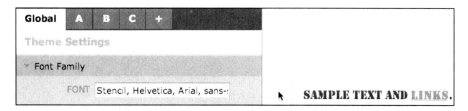

You can use the sliders (or enter values) in the **Corner Radii** area to change how much curvature is assigned to boxes and buttons. Again, your settings are previewed in the right-hand side window as you click outside a field.

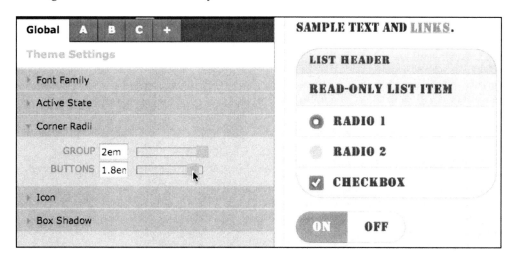

In the **Box Shadow** area, you can select a shadow color in the **COLOR** box; an opacity percentage in the **OPACITY** box (100 percent is the darkest shadow and 0 percent is no shadow); and a size (in pixels) in the **SIZE** box.

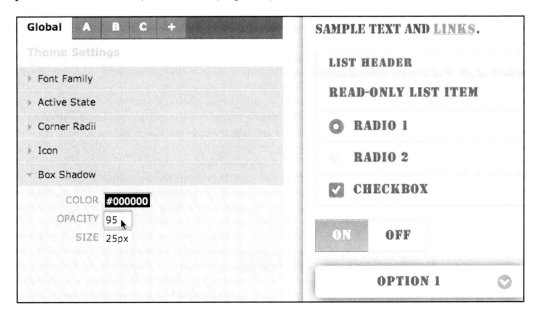

Defining custom swatches

A swatch is a set of formatting options within the stylesheet that defines jQuery Mobile sites. You can add as many as 26 custom color swatches to your custom theme. You can customize header, footer, and content styles as well as button state styles for each swatch.

Let's start with the process for creating one. As noted, you access the interface for defining the colors (and other attributes) for a specific swatch by choosing that swatch from the set of tabs in the upper-left corner of the **ThemeRoller** page.

To customize the header and footer, expand the **Header/Footer Bar** panel on the left-hand side of the **ThemeRoller** window. Perform the following steps to define a color swatch for header and footer bars:

1. Click on the **TEXT COLOR** swatch. Use the outer ring to click a color close to the one you want to apply to text in headers and footers, and use the inner gradient to fine-tune your selection. The color you click will translate into a hexadecimal value in the **TEXT COLOR** box, as shown in the following screenshot:

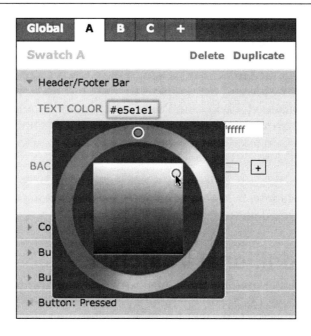

2. Text shadow serves to generate a subtle outline around text so that it shows more clearly. You are well served accepting the minimalist default settings (horizontal shadow, 0px; vertical shadow, 1px; blur, 1px; and color, white).

3. To set the background color, you can define a solid color (in the same way you defined text color in step 1). But gradient backgrounds are the stock-in-trade of mobile sites, so consider generating one. To do that, define a gradient by clicking on the plus (+) icon to the right-hand side of the **BACKGROUND** label, to expand the options. Choose a **START** and **END** color for the gradient, as shown in the following screenshot:

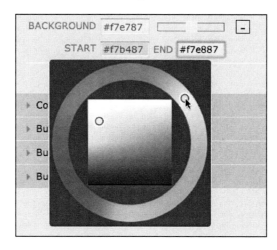

4. Defining colors for the content body area (that is, either areas covered by the `<body>` tag or the `<content>` element) is very similar to defining header or footer colors. The biggest difference is that you can define link state colors by expanding the **Link Color** section of the swatch. Click on the plus (+) icon next to **Link Color**, and define colors for each link state. You can define text color (and shadow), background color, and border color for three button states. The normal state displays when a button is not hovered over or pressed. Keep in mind that most mobile, and thus mouse-less mobile devices, can't fully take advantage of a hover state.

5. You can use the same techniques we've explored so far to define specific text color, text shadow, background color (or gradient), and borders for normal buttons, hovered buttons, and pressed buttons.

Creating additional swatches

By default, ThemeRoller presents three tabs that allow you to create and preview three different swatches (**A**, **B**, and **C**). Need more? To add more swatches, click on the **Add Swatch** link at the bottom of the ThemeRoller app window. Each time you do, new swatch panels are generated for swatches D, E, F, and so on—all the way to Z. You define these swatches the same way you defined swatches A-C.

Rolling a theme

Once you've created swatches and defined global attributes for your theme, perform the following steps to roll them into a theme and download them:

1. Click on the **Download** button at the top of the **ThemeRoller** screen. The **Download Theme** dialog opens. Enter `my-custom-theme` in the **Theme Name** field of the **Download Theme** dialog box.

2. Click on the **Download Zip** button.

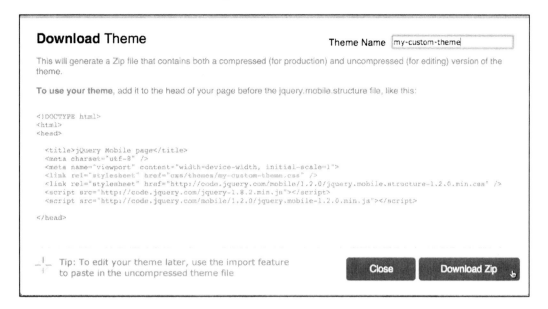

3. Your browser's download dialog box will appear. This will be different for different browsers and for Windows and Mac. Use the settings in the dialog box to save the file to the folder that defines your Dreamweaver site.

4. Finally, unzip the files. All the files we need are inside the **Themes** folder that gets unzipped.

Applying a custom theme in Dreamweaver

Now you're ready to apply the custom theme to your jQuery Mobile site.

The instructions for applying a ThemeRoller-generated CSS file that you might have noted in the **Download Theme** window (the one you used to create a ZIP file) are designed for folks who don't have Dreamweaver. The process is easier when you are working in Dreamweaver. All you have to do is attach the generated CSS file with -min at the end of the filename (but before the .css filename extension) to your jQuery Mobile site.

Perform the following steps to do that:

1. Back in Dreamweaver, view the **CSS Styles** panel and click on the **Attach Style Sheet** icon. The **Attach External Style Sheet** dialog opens.

2. Click on the **Browse** button in the **Attach External Style Sheet** dialog. The **Select Style Sheet File** dialog opens. Navigate, in your site folder, to the file with -min at end of the filename. Double-click on that file to link your jQuery Mobile page to this CSS file.

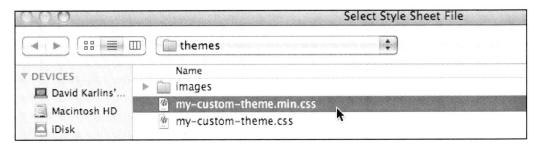

3. Click on **OK** in the **Attach External Style Sheet** dialog. Your custom CSS file is added to your original CSS file, and will apply your custom theme styling.

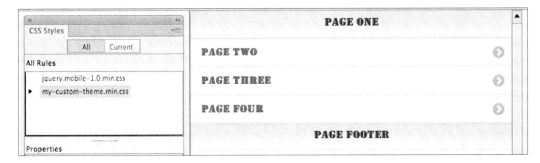

4. Click on the **Refresh** icon at the bottom of the **jQuery Mobile Swatches** panel to refresh the panel and display your custom swatches and theme attributes. With your **jQuery Mobile Swatches** panel reloaded with your own custom theme, you can use either the panel, or **Code** view, to apply your own custom data-themes to any element.

Summary

This chapter was a bit unusual in that we focused most of our attention outside of Dreamweaver, per se. In some ways, we can think of Dreamweaver as the conductor of an orchestra—in this case, drawing on and integrating custom themes to create really unique jQuery Mobile sites.

The ability to generate custom themes with ThemeRoller, and then integrate them into a Dreamweaver jQuery Mobile site is really a major event. It allows us to break free of the boring five-swatch options built into jQuery Mobile, and instead, access unlimited options for themes and color schemes.

As you build your own themes keep in mind that a single theme contains multiple swatches. Thus, your theme will define a set of standard elements (particularly a font family). And then you can build color swatches, as many as 26, that will be rolled into a single theme.

In the final chapter of this book, we'll discuss the PhoneGap online resource that generates full-scale apps. These apps run in mobile devices without browsers. And Dreamweaver CS6 includes substantial new tools to generate apps through PhoneGap without coding.

10
Building Apps with PhoneGap

What is an app? How do apps differ from mobile-friendly websites?

Do you need an app? How do you create apps in Dreamweaver?

In this chapter, we'll answer all those questions, and walk through, step-by-step, the process of creating an app in Dreamweaver CS6.

An **app**—short for application—differs from a mobile-friendly website in that an app does not run in a browser. Instead, an app functions as a standalone program that runs in a mobile device operating system. Freed from the constraints of running in a browser, apps can take advantage of the entire viewport of a mobile device. Also, apps can run on a mobile device even when the device is not connected to the Internet.

While in most ways, apps look and feel very much like jQuery Mobile pages, they are very different "under the hood." Apps are written in high-level programming languages, while mobile-friendly sites can be created with HTML5, CSS3, and JavaScript (the three components of jQuery Mobile).

With Dreamweaver CS5.5, Adobe introduced tools that allow you to convert a jQuery Mobile site into an app. Those app-generating tools are still in their early evolutionary stages. In fact, the features for generating apps in Dreamweaver CS6 have been scaled down a bit from those that were available in Dreamweaver 5.5. Nonetheless, you can generate real, working apps in Dreamweaver; and in this chapter, we will walk through how to do that.

The following topics are covered:

- Understanding the relationship between apps and mobile websites
- An overview of the two main mobile operating systems: Android and iOS
- Emulating apps on a PC
- Installing the Android Software Developers Kit
- Using PhoneGap with Dreamweaver
- Configuring PhoneGap settings
- Generating apps with Dreamweaver
- Testing and distributing apps

Apps and mobile websites

As briefly noted in the introduction to this chapter, apps (applications) are full-fledged software programs. One major implication of this is that apps need to work on a specific operating system. Dreamweaver, for example, is an app (application). Dreamweaver runs on two operating systems: Microsoft Windows and Apple's OS X operating system. And again, apps are specific to an operating system, so you can't run the Windows version of Dreamweaver on a Mac (nor can you run the Mac version of Dreamweaver on a Windows machine). And neither the Mac nor the Windows version of Dreamweaver runs on a Linux machine.

The point? When you create apps for mobile devices, you have to create separate versions of your app for each mobile operating system. There are many mobile operating systems, including Google Android, Apple iOS, Microsoft's Windows Phone, HP's WebOS, Blackberry, and Symbian.

The dominant mobile operating systems that serve between them, the overwhelming majority of mobile devices, are Android and iOS.

Android and iOS

Google sponsored the development of, and later purchased the Android mobile operating system. Android is open source—meaning that anyone can access the source code. And Google's approach has been to encourage mobile manufacturers to use Android as the operating system on their devices. At this point in the development of mobile devices, the Android operating system is found on a very wide array of mobile devices, from Amazon's Kindle Fire, Samsung's tablets and smart phones, and low-cost smart phones available for as little as $39. Android is the most widely used mobile operating system.

The large audience for Android apps has given rise to hundreds of thousands of apps for Android. The largest distributor of Android apps is the Google Play online marketplace, but Android apps can be distributed by anyone as files with the .apk filename extension.

You can build an Android app and e-mail it to clients or friends, or make it available from your website. That is the scenario we will focus on in this chapter.

Apple's iOS mobile operating system is not open source. iOS is only available on iPhones, iPads, Apple TV, and on the iPod Touch.

Just as Apple tightly controls access to the iOS operating system, so too does it tightly control the distribution of apps that run on iOS. Distributing iOS apps requires getting your app placed in the iTunes store, and an approval by Apple. That process is complicated—and even political.

 Apple argues that the strict control it places on what apps can be marketed through iTunes ensures quality control. Apple's critics point to incidents such as the banning in 2009 of a cartoon app called *NewsToons* by Pulitzer prize winning cartoonist Mark Fiore, on the grounds that it "ridiculed" public figures. In the wake of widespread protests, Apple reversed its decision and allowed the *NewsToons* app to be marketed through iTunes.

To avoid getting bogged down in the procedure for becoming an approved iOS app developer, we'll focus on generating and distributing Android apps with Dreamweaver in this chapter. That said, if you are an approved Apple iOS app developer, the steps for building iOS apps are almost identical to those for building Android (and other) apps, so you'll have no trouble adding an iOS version of your app using the step-by-step instructions later in this chapter.

Understanding PhoneGap

PhoneGap is a mobile development framework developed with support from, and now owned by Adobe. PhoneGap generates apps from pages created using JavaScript, HTML5, and CSS3, which means it can generate apps from jQuery Mobile pages.

PhoneGap can generate multiple apps from a single set of HTML, CSS, and JavaScript files. Earlier versions of PhoneGap (the version used in Dreamweaver CS5.5) could only generate iOS apps on OS X (Apple) computers, but the current version uploads files to the cloud, where they are converted to apps, and so you can create iOS apps from a Windows computer.

PhoneGap can be accessed and used without Dreamweaver (at www.phonegap.com), but Dreamweaver provides a simplified, more accessible set of tools for generating apps with PhoneGap directly from Dreamweaver.

Before building apps

Billy Joel has a song with the following line:

> *"Have you heard about the new style, honey? All you need is looks and a whole lot of money."*

You don't need either looks or a whole lot of money to build apps in Dreamweaver, but there are two things you do need:

1. A working jQuery Mobile page. The previous three chapters in this book walk you through the process of building jQuery Mobile websites, so if you dived into this book here, you'll want to backtrack a few chapters to pick up the skills you need to create jQuery Mobile sites.

2. A PhoneGap Build service account. Dreamweaver actually serves as a frontend, so to speak, for PhoneGap. But Dreamweaver will ask you to log into your PhoneGap account. I'll walk you through the process of acquiring a PhoneGap account and login info shortly.

There is a third element that is useful, but not essential to building apps in Dreamweaver CS6, and that is the **Software Developer Kit** (**SDK**) for Android (and, if you are a registered iOS developer, you can download an SDK for iOS as well). The SDK allows you to preview, and test your app on your own computer, so let's walk through the process of downloading those files as well.

Creating a PhoneGap Build service account

Let me emphasize: You cannot use PhoneGap Build and Dreamweaver without a PhoneGap Build service account. Accounts are free and easy to set up. To create one, visit the PhoneGap Build website at `https://build.phonegap.com/people/sign_up`.

When you get to the PhoneGap Build website, you'll see two options for registering. One of those options is with an Adobe ID. If you already have an Adobe ID, you can use it here, if not, you can create one.

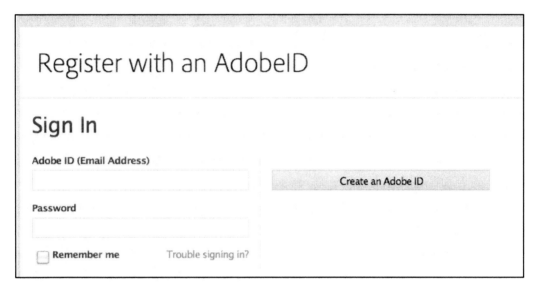

Downloading the Android SDK

While the Android SDK is not necessary to build apps, it is necessary to preview and test apps on your own computer. Also the SDK is free and easy to download, and helpful in previewing and testing apps, so you should download it.

To download the set of files that comprise the Android SDK, go to
`http://developer.android.com/sdk`. Click on the **Download the SDK** button as shown in the following screenshot:

Clicking on the **Download the SDK** button takes you to a legal page. Read the terms and conditions, check the **I have read and agree with the above terms and conditions** checkbox, and click on the **Download the SDK** button (exact wording differs depending on your operating system).

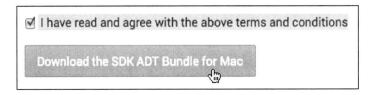

When you click the **Download** button, the download begins. Save the ZIP file to a folder where you will be able to find it. Unzip the file—the Mac version is `adt-bundle-mac-x86_64.zip`, the Windows version a bit different.

Here's the important thing: Save the unzipped files, there is a folder named `SDK`. Keep track of where that folder is in your computer's file structure. You'll need to navigate to this folder in Dreamweaver during the process of configuring the PhoneGap build feature.

PhoneGap and Dreamweaver

You're going to find that 99 percent of the work of generating apps in Dreamweaver, using PhoneGap, is done before you start exporting your pages to apps. In short, it's all about preparation. If all your pieces are in place, generating apps is hassle-free.

A rule to keep in mind when you are preparing a jQuery Mobile page to be exported to an app: Every app has to be based on a distinct Dreamweaver site. To put it another way, you can't build two different apps from files in the same Dreamweaver site.

Throughout this book, I have emphasized the importance of always working in a Dreamweaver site. That rule takes on new importance when you are building a site that will be exported to an app.

It is, of course, very possible to create more than one jQuery Mobile HTML page in a single Dreamweaver site. And that's fine, as long as you're not planning on exporting that HTML page to an app. If, however, you plan on exporting your jQuery Mobile page to an app, create a new Dreamweaver site, and create only one HTML page in that site. Name the page `index.html`.

If you have saved your jQuery Mobile page as `index.html`, you're ready to use Dreamweaver's PhoneGap tools to export the content to an app.

Dreamweaver CS6 introduced substantially new and different procedures for generating apps. In some ways, the tools for generating apps in Dreamweaver CS5.5 were more powerful than those in CS6, but again, the steps are significantly different. For step-by-step instructions on generating apps in Dreamweaver CS5.5, see *Dreamweaver CS5.5 Mobile and Web Development with HTML5, CSS3, and jQuery, David Karlins, Packt Publishing.*

Configuring PhoneGap settings

You can generate apps in Dreamweaver without configuring PhoneGap settings. But you can't emulate the app in your computer unless and until you configure PhoneGap settings. Here's where you're going to need to remember where you saved those Android SDK files. Remember? Good, then you're ready to configure PhoneGap settings so you can emulate (preview and test) your Android app.

To do that, perform the following steps:

1. With your Dreamweaver site open, navigate to **Site | PhoneGap Build Service | PhoneGap Build Settings**. The **PhoneGap Build Settings** panel opens.

2. In the **Android** section of the panel (the top), click on the **Select a Location** (folder) icon and navigate to and select the **SDK** folder within the folders you unzipped from the Android SDK download file.

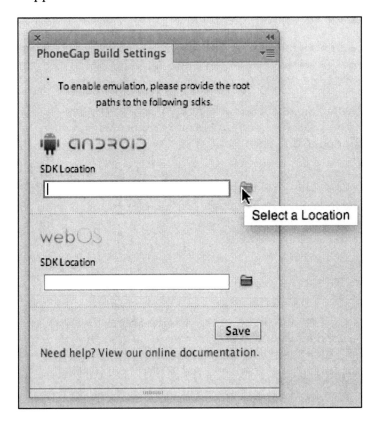

>
> Here, we are not addressing the installation procedure of the iOS SDK, but if you are a registered Apple developer, you can use the **Select a Location** (folder) icon, in the iOS section of the panel, and navigate to and select the folder into which you saved the unzipped iOS SDK files.

3. After you define PhoneGap SDK settings, click on the **Save** button in the **PhoneGap Build Settings** panel.

With your PhoneGap Build settings defined, you can emulate (test) your app in your desktop or laptop computer. Again, this is not essential—you can still create and test apps in a mobile device and download them to your computer without configuring the PhoneGap Build settings. But you'll find the development and testing process more efficient if you can test your apps directly on the same computer that you use to run Dreamweaver.

Generating apps with Dreamweaver

Let's review the checklist of items that need to be in place before you can generate an app in Dreamweaver:

- You need to be registered with PhoneGap, and have a login ID and password.
- You need to have a jQuery Mobile page built and saved as `index.html`. And remember, every app needs its own Dreamweaver site.
- If you want to be able to emulate your app on your own computer, you need to at least download the Android SDK, unzip the files, and use the **PhoneGap Build Settings** panel to define the location of those files.

With those pieces in place, you're ready to generate an app. To do that, perform the following steps:

1. Navigate to **Site | PhoneGap Build Service | PhoneGap Build Service**. The **PhoneGap Build Service** panel appears.
2. To begin the process of creating a new app, leave the dropdown set to the default, **Create as a new project**, and click on the **Continue** button.

3. After you click on **Continue**, a new **PhoneGap Build Service** panel opens. Here, you have the option to enter keys and passwords for apps that you plan to distribute professionally. Keys and passwords are not required for apps that you will distribute yourself, and are generally not necessary unless you are developing apps on a commercial basis for large-scale sale. You can select **None** in the **Key** popup for Android.

 For details on obtaining a key and password for Android apps, see `http://developer.android.com/tools/ publishing/app-signing.html#cert`.

4. Click on the **Continue** button in the following panel:

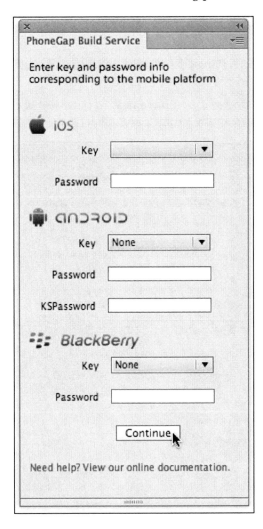

5. Yet another **PhoneGap Build Service** panel opens showing the progress of your apps being generated. There is nothing to do here but sit back, relax, and wait while PhoneGap generates your app(s).

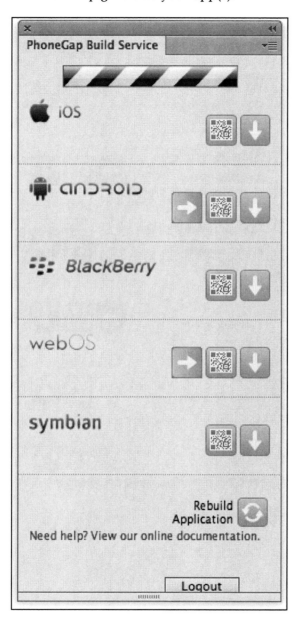

6. When PhoneGap is done generating apps for your configured mobile operating systems (which in our case means everything except iOS), the **PhoneGap Build Service** panel will display the status of each app.

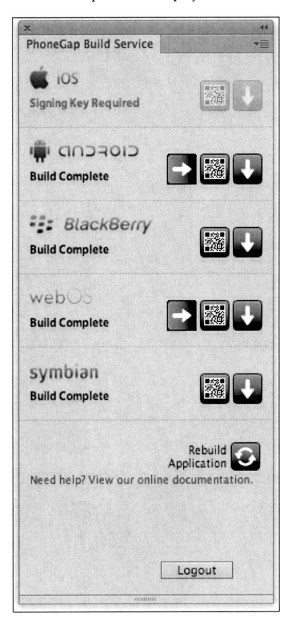

You are now ready to test and distribute your app(s). But don't close the **PhoneGap Build Service** panel! You'll need it to test and distribute your app.

Troubleshooting note

If the **PhoneGap Build Services** panel freezes repeatedly, the problem is likely not in your configuration or your Internet connection. Dreamweaver CS6 might have been shipped with what seems to have been an unacknowledged bug, and that resulted in the freezing of the **PhoneGap Build Services** panel. If this problem persists, navigate to **Help | Updates** in Dreamweaver, and update your Dreamweaver CS6 installation with the latest version, which will fix this bug.

Testing and distributing apps

There are three ways you can test apps before you distribute them:

- You can emulate the app on your computer, provided you downloaded and installed the SDK for that app.

- You can scan the app into a mobile device using that device's QR reader. That provides a link to the saved app file at the PhoneGap site and allows the app to be downloaded onto your mobile device for testing.

- You can download the app and transfer it from your computer to a mobile device.

Emulating an app on your own computer is the simplest of these options, and we'll focus on that. But I'll also walk through how to load your app into a mobile device with a QR reader, and how to download the app.

Testing apps with an emulator

The easiest way to see how your app will look in a mobile device is to emulate it on the desktop or laptop computer you use to run Dreamweaver. If you've installed and configured the SDK for any operating system (such as Android), that SDK includes emulation software.

To launch the emulator for any operating system, click on the **Emulate Application** icon in the **PhoneGap Build Service** panel.

The next screen that appears in the **PhoneGap Build Service** panel provides options (where they are operative) for how to emulate your app. Generally speaking, you will accept the default settings, and click on the **Launch** button.

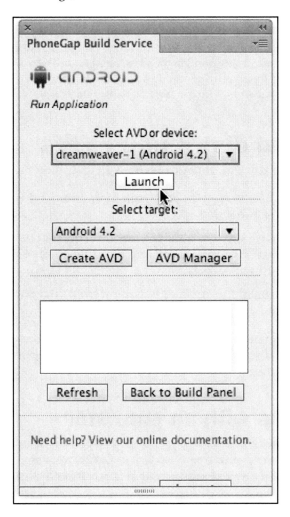

Launching an emulator requires an Internet connection, and takes some time. Why? Because the app is actually hosted at the PhoneGap site, and has to be downloaded from that site into the emulator window. So make sure you have a working Internet connection before launching an emulator, and be patient. Eventually, the emulator will launch, and you can test the app on your computer.

Different operating systems have different emulators, but they all provide both a keyboard and a preview window that displays your app more or less as it will appear and work on a mobile device.

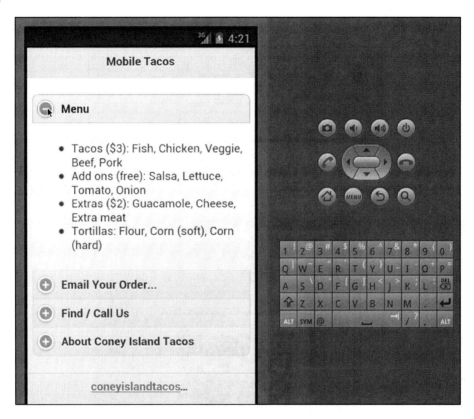

Revising your app

As a general rule, the testing and editing process for creating an app takes place before you generate the app. You want to make sure your jQuery Mobile site works the way you want it to when it gets transformed into an app.

That said, it is sometimes the case that when you test your app in an emulator window, you'll identify changes you need to make. You can do that by editing the jQuery Mobile site, and regenerating your app by clicking on the **Rebuild Application** icon at the bottom of the **PhoneGap Build Service** panel.

You can leave the emulator running during this process and update the emulator by clicking on the **Emulate Application** icon for your app. The app will need to be uploaded and regenerated, which takes substantial time—this emphasizes the importance of testing and perfecting your jQuery Mobile site before you generate apps.

Scanning apps into your Android device

Another way to test a generated Android app is to download it onto an Android device. To do that, click on the **View QR Code** icon for Android in the **PhoneGap Build Service** panel.

Once you click on the **View QR Code** icon, the **PhoneGap Build Service** panel displays a large, scanable QR code.

Using QR scanner software in an Android phone, scan the QR code into your Android device. You can do this by launching the QR Reader in your Android mobile device, and pointing the scan window at the QR code generated in Dreamweaver.

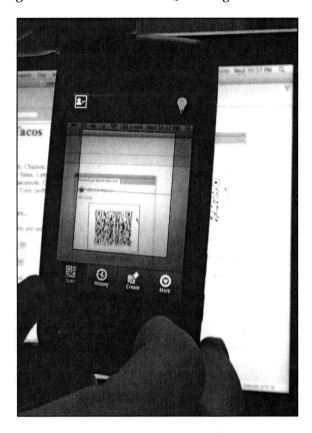

After you scan the QR code into your Android device, your device displays a link to the app file. Click on that link and use the tools in your Android device to download, open, and install the app file.

 A full exploration of how to download and install files on different Android mobile devices is beyond the scope of this book, but you can accomplish the entire process using Astro File Manager, an app that can be downloaded onto any Android mobile device.

Once you've downloaded and installed your app, you can test it on your Android mobile device. My own Android phone doesn't have a screen capture utility, so we'll have to use a photo of the screen to demonstrate how the app looks on my device.

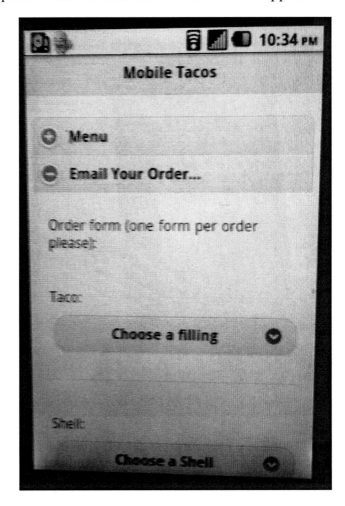

Downloading apps

The third option for testing your app is to download it onto your computer. The app won't run on your computer since it only runs on the mobile operating system for which it was created. But you can use any file transfer technique to move the file to your mobile device and test it.

Here again, we are straying well beyond Dreamweaver, but in general, you can transfer an app from your development computer to a mobile device by connecting your devices with a USB cord and dragging the app (which will have a `.apk` filename extension) onto your mobile device. You can then launch the app on your mobile device the same way you would launch any app.

Distributing Apps

App distribution is specific to each operating system. As noted, all apps for Apple devices are distributed through iTunes. Android apps are sold and distributed through Google Play. You do not need to be approved by Google to distribute apps through Google Play, but there are requirements, and you do have to register as an Android developer (and pay a registration fee). You'll find all the information you need to sell or distribute apps through Google Play at `https://play.google.com/apps/publish`.

While commercial distribution of apps is well beyond the scope of this book, you can distribute Android apps right from your website. Here's how to do that in Dreamweaver:

1. In the **PhoneGap Build Service** panel, click on the **Download Application** icon for Android.

2. The **Choose a Location to Save the .apk file** dialog opens. Navigate to the site through which you will be distributing the app, and click on the **Open** button to download your app to the selected folder. When the app is downloaded, a small dialog appears. Click on **OK** in that dialog.

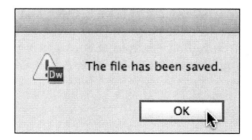

3. You can rename the app in Dreamweaver's **Local Files** panel, just be sure to keep the .apk filename extension.

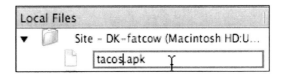

4. With the .apk file saved to a Dreamweaver site, you can create a link to that app file just as you would create a link to any other file.

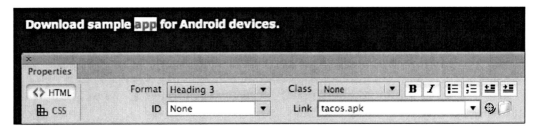

Distributing apps from your own site is an accessible, grassroots way to make your apps available. And given the technical limits of the kinds of apps you build through Dreamweaver, sharing apps from your website is an appropriate way to distribute them.

Summary

Apps are free-standing versions of your website. They do not require a browser to work on a mobile device, nor do they require an Internet connection (once they have been downloaded and installed). Apps are written in high-level programming language, and professional-level apps require substantial investment in high-level coding.

Dreamweaver CS6 partners with and serves as a frontend for the PhoneGap toolset. Those tools convert web pages built with HTML5, CSS3, and JavaScript (generally speaking, that means jQuery Mobile pages in Dreamweaver) into apps for a range of mobile operating systems including Android. If you are a registered Apple developer, you can use PhoneGap and Dreamweaver to create Apple iOS apps as well.

Dreamweaver CS6's PhoneGap Build Service manages the whole process of building, testing, and—on a simple level—distributing apps. Pages built with jQuery Mobile are uploaded to the PhoneGap server where they are converted to apps and saved.

You can test apps by using emulator software that is part of the Software Developer Kit (SDK) files provided by each operating system. You can distribute a generated app yourself by downloading the app file onto your computer, and publishing a link to the file in a web page, just as you would publish a link to any file.

Do Dreamweaver CS6's app tools rise to the level of creating commercially-distributed apps sold through Google Play or iTunes? Probably not. Apps built by professional coders will load more quickly, run faster, can include 3D graphics, and most importantly, can be customized for different operating systems (whereas PhoneGap generates apps for every operating system based on the same source files). But the apps you build in Dreamweaver work well enough to be distributed for free. And if you elect to contract with a professional coder to create a commercial-quality app, you can use your PhoneGap-generated app as a model for your coding team to work from.

Index

Thank you for buying
Dreamweaver CS6 Mobile and Web Development with HTML5, CSS3, and jQuery Mobile

About Packt Publishing

Packt, pronounced 'packed', published its first book *"Mastering phpMyAdmin for Effective MySQL Management"* in April 2004 and subsequently continued to specialize in publishing highly focused books on specific technologies and solutions.

Our books and publications share the experiences of your fellow IT professionals in adapting and customizing today's systems, applications, and frameworks. Our solution based books give you the knowledge and power to customize the software and technologies you're using to get the job done. Packt books are more specific and less general than the IT books you have seen in the past. Our unique business model allows us to bring you more focused information, giving you more of what you need to know, and less of what you don't.

Packt is a modern, yet unique publishing company, which focuses on producing quality, cutting-edge books for communities of developers, administrators, and newbies alike. For more information, please visit our website: www.packtpub.com.

Writing for Packt

We welcome all inquiries from people who are interested in authoring. Book proposals should be sent to author@packtpub.com. If your book idea is still at an early stage and you would like to discuss it first before writing a formal book proposal, contact us; one of our commissioning editors will get in touch with you.

We're not just looking for published authors; if you have strong technical skills but no writing experience, our experienced editors can help you develop a writing career, or simply get some additional reward for your expertise.

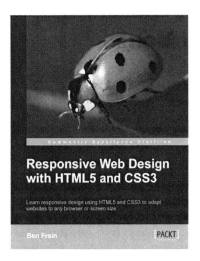

Responsive Web Design
with HTML5 and CSS3

Learn responsive design using HTML5 and CSS3 to adapt
websites to any browser or screen size

Ben Frain   PACKT

Responsive Web Design with HTML5 and CSS3

ISBN: 978-1-84969-318-9   Paperback: 324 pages

Learn responsive design using HTML5 and CSS3 to
adapt websites to any browser or screen size

1. Everything needed to code websites in HTML5
    and CSS3 that are responsive to every device or
    screen size

2. Learn the main new features of HTML5 and
    use CSS3's stunning new capabilities including
    animations, transitions, and transformations

3. Real world examples show how to
    progressively enhance a responsive design
    while providing fall backs for older browsers

Learn by doing. less theory, more results

WebGL

Become a master of 3D web programming in WebGL
and JavaScript

Beginner's Guide

Diego Cantor   Brandon Jones

WebGL Beginner's Guide

ISBN: 978-1-84969-172-7   Paperback: 376 pages

Become a master of 3D web programming in WebGL
and JavaScript

1. Dive headfirst into 3D web application
    development using WebGL and JavaScript.

2. Each chapter is loaded with code examples
    and exercises that allow the reader to quickly
    learn the various concepts associated with 3D
    web development

3. The only software that the reader needs to run
    the examples is an HTML5 enabled modern
    web browser. No additional tools needed.

4. A practical beginner's guide with a fast paced
    but friendly and engaging approach towards
    3D web development

Please check **www.PacktPub.com** for information on our titles

HTML5 Canvas Cookbook

ISBN: 978-1-84969-136-9   Paperback: 348 pages

Over 80 recipes to revolutionize the web experience
with HTML5 Canvas

1. The quickest way to get up to speed
   with HTML5 Canvas application and
   game development

2. Create stunning 3D visualizations and
   games without Flash

3. Written in a modern, unobtrusive, and objected
   oriented JavaScript style so that the code can be
   reused in your own applications.

Ext JS 4 Web Application
Development Cookbook

ISBN: 978-1-84951-686-0   Paperback: 488 pages

Over 110 easy-to-follow recipes backed up with
real-life examples, walking you through basic Ext
JS features to advanced application design using
Sencha's Ext JS

1. Learn how to build Rich Internet Applications
   with the latest version of the Ext JS framework
   in a cookbook style

2. From creating forms to theming your
   interface, you will learn the building blocks for
   developing the perfect web application

3. Easy to follow recipes step through practical
   and detailed examples which are all fully
   backed up with code, illustrations, and tips

Please check **www.PacktPub.com** for information on our titles

CPSIA information can be obtained at www.ICGtesting.com
Printed in the USA
BVOW06s0458150813

328325BV00013B/146/P

9 781849 694742